RHYME SPIN

Nursery Rhymes as a Springboard
to Christian Views

Steve Bradley

outskirts
press

Rhyme Spin
Nursery Rhymes as a Springboard to Christian Views
All Rights Reserved.
Copyright © 2020 Steve Bradley
v2.0

The opinions expressed in this manuscript are solely the opinions of the author and do not represent the opinions or thoughts of the publisher. The author has represented and warranted full ownership and/or legal right to publish all the materials in this book.

This book may not be reproduced, transmitted, or stored in whole or in part by any means, including graphic, electronic, or mechanical without the express written consent of the publisher except in the case of brief quotations embodied in critical articles and reviews.

Outskirts Press, Inc.
http://www.outskirtspress.com

ISBN: 978-1-9772-3043-0

Cover Photo © 2020 www.gettyimages.com. All rights reserved - used with permission.

Outskirts Press and the "OP" logo are trademarks belonging to Outskirts Press, Inc.

PRINTED IN THE UNITED STATES OF AMERICA

Does a rhymer rhyme? Does a chimer chime? Do you need a reason to rhyme? Is there a season to chime? Do you need a reason to chime? Is there a season to rhyme? There's a time to rhyme and a time to chime. If we are in a season with no reason, then it is time to chime. There is more reason to chime than there is to rhyme. No rhyme, no crime. No reason, chime season.

What does that mean? Is there a meaning to it? Could it be sarcasm or perhaps satire? Is there something suggestive? Does it allude to, and hint of anything specific, or is it nonsense? There is both rhyme and reason.

There is much familiarity with many old nursery rhymes. Catchy phrases and words put together using silliness, satire, or sarcasm, sometimes nonsense, to use as an educational tool. A teaching tool for children to teach them about past events. Many are effectively constructed to make them both easy to remember and easy to repeat.

By taking another look at some old and popular nursey rhymes maybe we can find both rhyme and reason, and perhaps we can find more. We will find plenty of rhyme, and with a closer look, a lot of reason behind most of the writings. Many were used as a teaching tool for children about past events. Hence, the label of nursery rhymes. Is it possible to use them in a similar way regarding current events?

The purpose of this writing is to take randomly selected words or phrases from the large assortment of nursery rhymes, or fairy tales and throw them into a huge mixing bowl. We will mix them up, pour them out, and see what comes out. Is it possible to put silliness, nonsense and reason into a mixing bowl and get something sensible and serious to come out? Something that pertains to current trends and events? Could something go in as childish or frivolous and come out serious and wise? Is it possible to use something that resonates to children about past events to find something that resonates to adults today? I think it is very possible. Let the spin begin.

Table of Contents

Jack And The Beanstalk..............................1
FOE...3
FEE...6
FIE...9
FUM..12
Hey Diddle Diddle..................................15
ITSY BITSY SPIDER..................................18
HUMPTY DUMPTY......................................23
THREE BLIND MICE...................................26
If Wishes Were Horses, Beggers Would Ride..........29
Hickory Dickory Dock...............................32
Row Row Row Your Boat..............................35
Jack and Jill......................................38
Jack Sprat...41

Mary Had A Little Lamb 45
Goosey Goosey Gander 49
Baa, Baa, Black Sheep 53
This Little Piggy 55
There Was An Old Woman Who Lived In A Shoe. 59
My Little Old Man 62
Little Miss Muffet 66
Tweedledee And Tweedledum 70
It's Raining It's Pouring 73
Pop Goes The Weasel. 76
A Tisket A Tasket. 79
I Had A Little Nut Tree 81
Oranges and Lemons 84
A Wise Old Owl 88
Miss Polly Had A Dolly 92
Hot Cross Buns 96
There Was an Old Lady Who Swallowed a Fly. 99
Jack Be Nimble 103
The Wheels On The Bus 107
I'm A Little Teapot. 109
Old MacDonald Had A Farm 112
A Pinch of Salt. 116
Mary, Mary, Quite Contrary 119

Little Jack Horner	123
Twinkle, Twinkle, Little Star	125
Blow Wind, Blow	128
Simple Simon	131
Old Mother Hubbard	134
Little Boy Blue	137
Hide and Seek	139
Happily Ever After	142

Jack And The Beanstalk

An English fairy tale about a young boy climbing a beanstalk and stealing things from a giant. A poor boy living with his widowed mother. His mother tells her son to take the cow to market because it was no longer producing milk. On that mission, Jack encounters someone claiming to have magic beans. He accepts the beans for payment for the cow, plants them and the beanstalk appears. Consistent throughout the following pages we will see that there is an uncertainty as to origin and meaning. Some lines may be in reference to something or someone specific, or they may be folly or nonsense.

Fee Fie Foe Fum is the familiar line used in this English fairytale about Jack, the beanstalk and the giant. It is a nonsense phrase designed to strike terror into the heart of the listener, a phrase originating from an angry giant who was the victim of young Jack. Smelling the blood of an Englishman and grinding bones to make bread may indeed describe and create fear in the listeners, especially if the audience was young children. A fairy tale, a story for children about magical beings and imaginary lands consists of a lot of nonsense. Is there a meaning to those words? Origin and meaning varies quite a bit with many nursery rhymes and fairy tales, as does the meaning of some of the words used within them. Can we interpret them as we like and attach our own meaning?

Let's break the opening line down a bit, take a closer look and see if we can make some sense out of it. It is my hope that after reading the following pages, you are not terror struck, but concerned, not fearful, but curious, not apathetic, but enlightened.

We are not going to go any further than the opening four words with this fairy tale. We are only interested in taking those four words, analyzing them, expounding on them, and perhaps using them for our own catchy opening line, or applying self interpretation to the mix. A different approach to do see what we can see, just like the bear did. You may recall, that is why the bear went over the mountain. Let's go over the mountain and see what we can see.

The words are nonsense and the phrase does not allude nor insinuate anything, but perhaps we can take a closer look. The spelling in many early English expressions is very arbitrary and there are many variations.   Fee, fa, foh, fum.   Fee, fi, fo, fum   Fie, fih, foh, fum   are just an example of many variants that have been printed over the years. Rather than look at all of them together, we will randomly take one at a time.

FOE

Where do you think you stand, if you were asked "are you good or bad, positive or negative, friend or foe?" I think it is safe to assume that most of us would choose good over bad, positive over negative, and friend over foe. It is quite normal to prefer good over bad and positive over negative, but did you know that almost every single one of us is a foe? That's right, whether you want to believe it or not, you are a foe.

The definition of a foe is enemy or opponent. You and me both stand in the way of, and put up a resistance to, and hider the natural flow of certain things that are necessities. We so easily become our worst enemy, our biggest foe. We do it without difficulty, almost effortlessly.

We complicate and make difficult the flow of things that we cannot live without. We obstruct the flow of our blood, we obstruct the flow of water, and we are experts at hindering and sometimes blocking the flow of " living water." We truly have become Flow Obstruction Experts of both blood and water. We cannot live without either one, yet we hinder the flow of both.

You may have noticed, an acronym for what we have become, Flow Obstruction Experts or FOE. I am a FOE, you are a FOE, we all are obstructionists.

Blood and water are two things that sustain life. The value of each cannot be estimated other than to say they are both priceless! They are both requirements for life. They must continue to flow. Without them we would parish, both physically and spiritually.

Water is a colorless and odorless substance all over the Earth. Approximately 70% of the Earth is made up of water and up to 60% of the human adult body is water. It is prevalent and essential to life. I believe we take it for granted because of its abundance, yet we are continually polluting it. We value it as a precious resource on the one hand and contribute to its impurity on the other. We have learned how to use it effectively by the use of dams and levees, locks and turbines. We have learned how to pollute it by industrial waste, sewage and wastewater, mining activities, marine dumping, oil leakage, fertilizers and pesticides, and on and on. The natural flow has definitely been interrupted and obstructed. We are the guilty ones, the flow obstruction experts. We can take a resource of such great value, something not to be wasted or treated carelessly, and do just that. We are careless and wasteful taking something so precious and polluting it, causing adverse change. We are a foe to the flow.

It is a shame that we are causing such harm and damaging our environment. Something so pristine and unspoiled slowly fading because of our self proclaimed expertise. Water is necessary to sustain life, so is blood.

Blood is the body fluid that delivers necessary substances like oxygen and nutrients to our cells. Man has become quite accomplished at inhibiting the flow of blood through poor diet choices, bad habits and a lack of adequate exercise. We could not survive without water and we could not survive without blood. Both our physical and spiritual lives depend upon both.

We know the importance of both in regard to our physical life. There exists a great significance of both regarding our spiritual life as well. Christ's blood was shed for the salvation of mankind and the Holy Spirit is the Living Water. Man has become a master of denying and rejecting both. Our bodies are a temple where God's Spirit resides, if we let Him in. Our Flow Obstruction Expertise insists upon making different arrangements, hindering the flow of each.

FEE

We are all familiar with this word. It is a payment made in exchange for advice or services of some kind. It would be very easy to think of several kinds of fees and several instances where fees are charged. In the physical world in which we live, fees are routine, commonplace and customary worldwide, an everyday occurrence. Is there a fee in our spiritual world?

It is too easy to ignore the spiritual aspect of our lives. Getting caught up in the busyness of our lives makes it easy to concentrate only upon the physical. There are too many convenient excuses readily available, offered by many to justify ignoring the reality of the spiritual world. We can be so overwhelmed with the demands of our lives that we effortlessly cast aside any thought of putting more upon our plates. We can be so obsessed with survival and self that we refuse to acknowledge or even take notice of the existence of a spiritual life. We are body, soul, and spirit but many put on blinders and only see body, the physical component, while ignoring the spirit and soul. That mindset is very troublesome in the eternal scheme of things.

Our lives upon Earth are short. Take a moment to think about someone living to the age of 100. We would be quick to say that a person reaching 100 years of age lived a long life. When we compare those 100 years to forever, 100 years is not very long at all. It is important to realize that we are spending too much time concentrating upon the temporary and not enough time concentrating upon that which lasts forever. Physically we last here temporarily, spiritually we live eternally.

We need to get things in order and open our eyes to the Truth. You may ask "how does this have anything to do with fees?" Let me see if I can put it into simple terms.

A fee, as previously noted, is a payment made in exchange for something. In exchange for the salvation of man, a price was paid. Jesus, God incarnate, paid the ultimate price by dying on the cross for us. A price had to be paid for sin. Reading in the book of 1 Corinthians 6:20 we are told that "you have been bought with a price." That price was the blood of Christ. Our God is a just God and a price must be paid for sin, all sin. By being a just God means He acts according to what is morally right and fair.

Acting unjustly would be like a judge letting some who committed a crime off scot free and finding another that committed the same crime guilty. Our God is just and demands payment for sin. The "fee" or payment for sin has been made. Let's take a look at what scripture tells us. In the book of Romans chapter 3 verse 25 we see where Christ "whom God displayed publicly as a propitiation in His blood through faith". God publicly displayed His Son on Calvary for everyone to see. The death of Christ paid the price, satisfied the offended holiness and wrath of God against sinners, those who Christ died for.

The fee, or payment made by the death of Christ does not mean that since the price has been paid sin can abound and everyone is "home free". The sacrifice of Jesus on the cross satisfied our Holy God's demand for punishment of sin.

The first two verses of the book of 1 John reads: "My little children, I am writing these things to you so that you may not sin. And if anyone sins, we have an Advocate with the Father, Jesus Christ the righteous, and He Himself is the propitiation for our sins, and not for ours only, but also for those of the whole world." The pardon for sin is offered to the whole world but it is very important to understand that the pardon is only received by those who believe. In the gospel of John we read (John 14:6) "I am the way, the truth, and the life. No one comes to the Father except through me".

We have an advocate in Jesus. He will help us and in a modern sense act as a defense attorney. The key question is who will he represent? The answer can be found in one of the most familiar scriptures in the Bible, John 3;16. "For God so loved the world, that He gave His only begotten Son, that whosoever believes in Him shall not perish, but have eternal life".

FIE

The word fie, pronounced like pie, is used to express outrage or disgust. I think an entire book could be written about things that are outrageous or disgusting. What one finds disgusting may not be seen in the same way by another. There are some things that should be disgusting to all, but are not. The latter is what we should be concerned about.

Acts of terror, homicide, genocide all disgusting. The ideology of Hitler or Osama Bin Laden, the likes of Ted Bundy or Jeffrey Dahmer horrendous and appalling. They will always be considered disgusting and outrageous sparking profound disapproval.

There are several things that were once on the disgusting and disapproval list that have switched sides. What was at one time on the unacceptable list finds itself on the acceptable list. I find that disgusting. There has been an erosion process of our morals and values that has been going on for years. The voices that see it and shout it out are becoming outnumbered and are quickly outshouted. The times, they are a changin' is seen by many as progress. It is true that things change, progress is made in many areas. Not all changes are good changes. Many reflect the snowballing ideology of absolute freedom. Anarchy is a state of disorder due to the absence of authority. Where authority does exist, it fades by the increasing refusal to acknowledge it.

Where there is no order, there is disorder. Where there are no rules everything is unruly. Where there are no controls everything is out of control. We are not far from finding ourselves in that chaotic state. We will be there with just a little more "progress". This trend is what I find disgusting. Ignorance is not bliss. Ignorance is ignorance.

The authority figure that is missing is God. We are adrift, moving further and further away from Him. His absence in the hearts of mankind creates a void quickly filled by a rapidly expanding self. We are so quick to self appoint ourselves as chief operating officer. In a previous writing I expressed the remedy for such a doomsday course we insist upon traveling. The restoration of a nation begins with the restoration of the hearts of its people. The erosion is real and so is the recommended prescription for the cure. We need a larger dosage of God in our lives and a smaller dosage of self.

The longer we stay on the same course, the further away from God we get. Our direction has a destination. It is only when we come to the realization of how we are drifting away from God that we can take the necessary steps to get on the right course. Allowing God into our lives is the corrective action to take. Don't let "progress" stand in your way. Right is right and wrong is wrong. Interchanging them, or redefining them is the result of ignorance and denial. The times "they are a changin'". A determination needs to be made of

FIE

what is right and what is wrong. The direction we go rides in the balance. You too should be concerned and disgusted with the trend we are following. I repeat, our direction has a destination.

FUM

Like many words, there are multiple definitions and usages for the word fun. It is actually a legitimate scrabble word. Among the various definitions of this word are smoke, a mythological Chinese bird, and, to play upon a fiddle. Hey diddle diddle, I think we should stick to the fiddle although there is the possibility of using all three.

A person just wasting time, not paying attention to the things he or she should be paying attention to, could be referred to as one doing nothing of value and just fiddling around. If that same person did more than just waste time, and also spend a lot of time using deception, or creating a smoke screen to deceive and hide something in the process, I think it is safe to say that that person would be considered a double fummer. Is there anything else worse than a double fummer? I do believe there is.

What if that same person that fiddled around wasting time was deceptive, creating a smoke screen to hide multiple things and had some very different or bizarre ideas that were insisted upon and considered ridiculous? It is very possible that this person has "lost it" or that his or her mental capacity has "flown the coop". Birds fly the coop, even Chinese mythological birds called fum. In this scenario, we definitely have a triple fummer!

How many multiple fummers are there? The answer to that question is that there are millions. What would a fummer free environment look like? Does it even exist?

We all waste time, many are very cunning and deceptive, some have seemingly flown the coop. We are all guilty of having flaws and imperfections, some more than others. We all have strengths and weaknesses. Wouldn't it be nice if we could maximize our strengths and minimize our weaknesses? Increase the positive in our lives and decrease the negative? Maintain an inner peace even when our efforts fall short? Have something solid to stand upon rather than something unstable and crumbling? The answer is yes to all.

Yes to all because of the Truth. "On Christ the solid rock I stand, all other ground is sinking sand". "My hope is built on nothing less than Jesus' blood and righteousness." To those who believe those words, the answer to the questions asked above is a resounding yes. Unfortunately we are living in a world where there are far too many who would answer those questions quite differently. The reason they would answer differently is because they have not experienced and felt the reality of it.

Trying to explain the feeling that a new parent feels upon the birth of their first child is not the same as experiencing it for yourself. Just like painting a picture is not the same as being there and seeing in person what is being painted. Surrendering our lives to Christ and being born again, experiencing the reality of God being alive ,having an inner peace that only comes from His Spirit dwelling within us cannot adequately be explained. Experiencing it and telling about it are not the same. Nothing can take the place of reality. A notional idea of that feeling is no where like the experiencing the realness of it.

It is time to readjust our priorities, stop wasting time by fiddling around, and make a more concentrated effort to sharing the reality of what we know is Truth.

Hey Diddle Diddle

An old English nursery rhyme going back as far as the sixteenth century and maybe earlier. A cat playing a fiddle was a popular image, and many references were made to it. "Cat and the Fiddle" was also thought to be a common name for inns.

Hey diddle diddle we just talked about the fiddle as it related to Fum, but the question arises, did the cow really jump over the moon? Probably not, it would have taken an extremely exceptional cow. Maybe he was elated and over joyed because more people were eating chicken.

Silly nonsense really, but there is a meaning to "over the moon". It is an old English expression meaning extremely happy, being delighted or thrilled. The definition of joy is a feeling of great happiness and pleasure.

Highly unlikely that anyone will be jumping over the moon anytime soon, but the fact remains, the world could use more joy. There are multiple sources of joy depending upon what makes you happy. There are also different levels of joy, the highest being " over the moon." There are sixteen Bible verses about joy that are a good reminder of the natural beauty of life. Natural beauty is unblemished and not altered, changed or modified. Real joy is natural, a state of mind, an orientation of the heart. (Theopedia). What does that mean? Orientation is all about the direction you're facing. A political orientation is your political outlook. A job orientation is directing one in the direction chosen by the employer. Orientation of the heart is where your heart is, its direction. In order to obtain natural joy, the heart must be in the direction of God, the unblemished, unaltered, and pure one true God.

Many songs have been written about joy. The first one that comes to mind for me, and probably the most popular worldwide is Joy To The World. The explanation of why there is joy to the world follows. The Lord is come, let Earth receive her King. The words written by Isaac Watts was, at one time, and probably still is, the most published Christmas hymn in North America. The words are based on Psalm 98 and Psalm 96:11-12 which reads: "Let the heavens be glad, and let the earth rejoice; Let the sea roar, and all it contains." First published in the year 1719, it is filled with so much truth and reason to sing.

"He rules the world with truth and grace," and "Let ev'ry heart prepare Him room," and "heaven and nature sing." The song is loaded with so much truth and so many expressions of joy, it is no wonder it is so popular. If there was something that would propel us over the moon, it would be singing this song and feeling the power behind the words. It is a joyous celebration. Celebrating the coming of the King, Jesus, God incarnate, and the sovereignty, the supreme power and authority of God.

That joyous celebration could be shared by all, but it is not. It is shared by those whose hearts have prepared Him room and let Him in. Those who have not prepared a room in their hearts and let Him in cannot grasp the magnitude of peace and joy that He brings into our hearts. It is once again, a feeling that cannot be adequately explained.

I do believe the joy of salvation and having God's Spirit dwelling within takes peace and joy to a level only reached by the reality of those events in our lives. Over the moon and beyond!

ITSY BITSY SPIDER

If a cow can jump over the moon, certainly an itsy bitsy spider can climb up a waterspout. The cow did not seem to have much trouble accomplishing his task, but the little spider did. I guess some things are easier for some than they are for others. We have already looked at the conditions necessary for the cow to be successful, but what about the itsy bitsy spider?

I'm sure for a tiny little spider, the job ahead was very challenging, requiring a lot of determination and perseverance. He needed to stay focused in order to be successful. There is a lesson to be learned there.

Many successful people throughout history encountered multiple failures before achieving success. The likes of Thomas Edison, Henry Ford, and even Ray Kroc to mention a few. A famous quote from Henry Ford is worth mentioning here because, at least the first part, describes the attitude of this little spider. "Failure is simply the opportunity to begin again, this time more intelligently". We cannot question the determination of the itsy bitsy spider, but were the multiple attempts at climbing up the waterspout done any differently?

ITSY BITSY SPIDER

Was anything learned, or was there any indication of making each attempt more intelligently than the previous?

We have all heard the definition of insanity. In case you haven't, it goes something like this: doing the same thing over and over again and expecting different results. I do not want to be accused of claiming the itsy bitsy spider was insane, but his actions speak for themselves.

I am going to give the little guy the benefit of the doubt and say that his actions were perfectly normal and also make an observation as to why he was not successful on his many attempts at climbing that downspout. I think it is pretty obvious, but let's take a closer look.

The itsy bitsy spider made progress and moved forward only when the sun came out from behind the clouds. When the rain came back the sun was again blocked by the clouds and down came the spider. This happened time and time again.

Is it safe to assume that when the sun was in full view, and the clouds were absent, the result was success in moving forward? The answer is yes, over, and over, and over again. The sun made the conditions favorable for the little guy to succeed. In the absence of the sun, the rain came, and his footing was unstable. Things became slippery and he was unable to hold firmly, down he went.

There is definitely a lesson to learn from itsy bitsy. We just need to make a comparison and use an analogy here. When we use the analogy. we will see that the itsy bitsy example turns into something of extreme importance. From itsy bitsy to life changing. This will be made evident when we make one simple change in spelling and put ourselves in place of the spider. We need to also change the task from climbing up the downspout to the task of navigating our walk through life.

The sun played a significant role with the spider in determining his success climbing the downspout. The Son has a paramount role in determining life. The spider was itsy bitsy. The Son is bigger than we can imagine. The spider was limited, the Son is not. The Son, as part of the triune God created the sun.

One God in three persons, Father, Son, and Holy Spirit. The trinity is not 1+1+1=3 , but 1x1x1=1. There are many scriptures to support the fact that all three persons are the Creator. I will share only two.

To begin with, pun intended, we read in the first book of Genesis, verse 1:26 to be specific, "Then God said, Let us make man in Our image, according to Our likeness….." The "Us" and "Our" referred to here are the Father, Son, and Holy Spirit.

Paul writes in the book of Colossians about the Preeminence of Christ. In verse 16 of chapter 1 we read: " For by Him all things were created, both in the heavens and on earth, visible and invisible, whether thrones or dominions or rulers or authorities   all things have been created through Him and for Him".

The Son really did create the sun. Suddenly the itsy bitsy spider looks more like the infinitesimal or microscopic spider! So small, not noticed, not recognizable, ignored, overlooked, neglected and undiscovered. Life goes on as if itsy bitsy doesn't even exist.

By comparison, the creator of the universe, the omnipresent, omnipotent, and omniscient God gets the same exact kind of treatment, ignored, overlooked and neglected. How is that possible? Priorities need to be adjusted and we need to refocus. Our focus is on ourselves, exclusively on me, myself, and I. We have prioritized the wrong trio. Life is much better when we include the Father, Son, and Holy Spirit. Our concentration of attention needs to be adjusted, regularly.

A proper focus needs to be maintained. How and what we focus on makes all the difference in the world, or should I say universe. I cannot stress enough the importance of concentration and focus. Let me share an example of that importance.

When we revisit the scriptural account of Peter coming out of the boat and walking on water, what changed to make Peter begin to sink? He was walking toward Jesus then "But seeing the wind, he became frightened, and beginning to sink, he cried out, Lord save me". (Matthew 14:29-30) The answer is obvious, Peter lost his focus upon Jesus and began to sink. What happens when we as followers of Christ get distracted because the winds and waves pick up. We lose our focus, we get distracted and begin to sink, pulled by the underlying current of ignorance, neglect and denial and blown off course by the prevailing winds of deception and misinformation.

We all have challenges, we face hurdles and detours, obstacles to avoid and hills or mountains to climb, it is a part of life. How we navigate those things depends upon our focus.

The little spider was trying to make it up the downspout. Many have lost focus and spend their lives trying to make it up their own self built beanstalk, thinking that there is a magical pot of gold that will be the solution to all of their problems. We need to realize that whatever we are trying to create or build, whatever we are trying to accomplish, whatever we are trying to climb, we must maintain focus upon the Son, the Word, the Truth.

More words of wisdom from the scriptures. Matthew 6: 19-21 says, Do not store up for yourselves treasures on earth, where moth and rust destroy, and where thieves break in and steal. But store up for yourselves treasures in heaven, where neither moth nor rust destroys, and where thieves do not break in or steal; for where your treasure is, there your heart will be also".

Where is your treasure? Where is your heart? Stay focused, but use wisdom when deciding upon what you focus on. The sun was needed by an itsy bitsy spider, the Son is needed by the whole world.

From tiny itsy bitsy to big and lumpy humpty dumpty. Let's take a closer look at Humpty Dumpty.

HUMPTY DUMPTY

The average person doesn't know much about this fictitious character. Most believe him to be an egg that shattered when he fell off of the wall. There are other beliefs or views about the meaning of Humpty Dumpty. They vary from a boiled ale or brandy, a dumpy clumsy or large person, an egg and even a canon.

The most popular belief currently is that of an egg, dumpy and large, and so clumsy that he took a great fall and broke into many pieces. No one seems to know who or what Humpty Dumpty was. There is also a belief that Humpty Dumpty was a large, powerful canon that was used in the English Civil War. This canon was put on the roof of a church that was known as "St Mary's by the wall". The wall was built to protect the city of Colchester. In one of the battles the gun tumbled down, shattered, and could not be raised again, it took a great fall.

There is also the belief that Humpty Dumpty referred to Charles 1 of England himself. He was toppled by a Puritan majority in Parliament, his great fall, and the kings army was unable to make it possible for him to regain power.

All three accounts of what Humpty Dumpty refers to have one thing in common, there was a great fall for each. The egg fell, the canon fell and so did the king. All three were unable to regain their position before the great fall, there was no restoration or restitution made.

There was another fall that did not just change a single egg, did not just change the condition or where abouts of a canon, and did not just change just the life of one person. I am talking about the fall of man, the fall, the term used in Christianity to describe the transition of the first man and first woman, Adam and Eve. We read about this in the third chapter of the book of Genesis. Adam and Eve underwent a transition from innocent obedience to a state of guilty disobedience.

The fall of man changed things for all of mankind. Unlike the three examples of a fall previously mentioned, there was restoration made for the fall of man. Man was separated from God by sin. Jesus Christ bridged that gap by His sacrifice and by the propitiation for our sins. "He is the propitiation for our sins, and not for ours only but also for the sins of the whole world" (1 John 2:2)

One trespass, the fall of man, disobeying God, affected everyone, but the sacrifice made by Jesus, dying on the cross for the benefit of mankind, satisfied the penalty for sin for all. Look at Romans 5:18, "So then as through one transgression there resulted condemnation to all men, even so through one act of righteousness there resulted justification of life to all men". There is one God and there is one mediator between God and man. The mediator is God incarnate, the Son of God, Jesus. (1 Timothy 2:5)

The act of disobedience that resulted in the fall of man was the eating of the forbidden fruit from the tree of knowledge in the garden of Eden. Mankind chooses to continue eating from that tree rather than to be fed by the Word of God. The result of that choice is to be misled, misinformed and blinded to the Truth.

THREE BLIND MICE

Were the three blind mice blinded to the truth? One account of the meaning of this rhyme is that during the Catholicism and Protestant conflict, the three blind mice were three Protestants executed by Queen Mary I of England. Another belief is that the three blind mice refer to three decrepit rodents whose vision was impaired, pursuing a farmers wife and getting their tails cut off in the process.

A young child pays more attention to the catchy rhythm than the actual meaning of the words in many cases regarding nursery rhymes. The reason behind the writing of many is seldom understood by the young reciting the words repeatedly. In today's political correct world, discretion should be used when choosing a nursery rhyme. Other opinions as to the meaning of this rhyme exist. I have only mentioned a couple. There are some people who question whether three blind mice is a children's song or a lesson in violent revenge. Isn't it incredible that so many different opinions can come from the same place? I believe many simply see what they want to see and make their own conclusions, based upon the color of lenses they choose to look through.

We can draw the conclusion that we want and claim it to be sound and factual just to justify any action we want to take. Isn't that really a form of blindness? The Queen of England, a catholic, believed differently than the protestants and claimed those not sharing her belief were blind. The protestants, firm in their belief were convinced that it was the Queen and the catholic believers who were the blind ones.

The three blind mice were actually given names. In the Homelands the names were, Leland, Prescott, and Thaddeus. In Shrek they were, Forder, Gorder, and Horder. I am going to name them something even different. The three, with impaired vision, or total blindness will be named, Left, Right, and Tweener. All three have quite a following. They all believe the other two, not sharing their own beliefs, are the blind ones. There are members in each camp that have impaired vision, some totally blind. Many are in darkness and need to be enlightened. Many enlightened need to be realigned.

Whether you are Left, Right, or somewhere in between, there will be impaired vision and blindness. The only way to avoid it is to have the eyes of your heart enlightened. (Ephesians 1:18) In the gospel of John, chapter 16 verse 13 more clarity is given: "When the Spirit of Truth comes, He will guide you into all truth…." To become enlightened and find truth we must ask, seek, and knock. (Matthew 7:7-8)

To refuse, ignore and deny the truth is ignorance and blindness. The source of truth, righteousness and all that is good comes only from God. Sunglasses are tinted to protect the eyes from sunlight or glare. We can choose any tint of glasses we want. Why is there an insistence by many, to look through lenses that protect the eyes from Son light and Truth?

There is more at stake than just having our tails cut off. Three blind mice, see how they run. How our lives are run and who they are run by is critical, crucial, and consequential. Seek and find the Truth.

My favorite scripture is Proverbs 3:5-6. I am going to include verse 7: "Trust in the Lord with all your heart And do not lean on your own understanding, In all your ways acknowledge Him, And He will make your paths straight. Do not be wise in your own eyes; Fear the Lord and turn away from evil".

There is an insistence on trying to be wise in our own eyes. That only results in impaired vision at best, and leads to total blindness, willful blindness. We can show a stubborn and determined intention to do as we want, regardless of the consequences. Open your eyes and see the light. Do not be deceived or misled by blind guides. "If a blind man guides a blind man, both will fall into a pit." (Matthew 15:14) You cannot let your light shine if you have not been enlightened. Three blind mice, see how they run. Take a look at how you run. Do you lack perception, awareness, or discernment? Are you unable to see, or do you only see what you want to see? Are you unable to see or just unwilling? Is there a turning of a blind eye, ignoring information as if it does not exist?

The unbelievers mind has been blinded. (2 Corinthians 4:4) Without a Godly influence man will follow the world system created by the adversary, blinded from the light of the gospel, the good news. The good news of Jesus and salvation. The lack of enlightenment deepens the moral darkness and the blind mice continue to run.

If Wishes Were Horses, Beggers Would Ride

First recorded in 1628, a shorter title of "If Wishes Were Horses" appeared much later. Unlike many nursery rhymes, there is a certainty to this one. Simply put, if wishing could make things happen, everyone, including beggers, would saddle up and everyone would have everything they need. Everyone would hop on and ride anywhere and receive anything. You could receive everything you would ever want or need, wishes would come true.

Wishful thinking is where your beliefs and your decision making is based on imagination, not on evidence, rationality, or reality. Things only happen in your imagination, not in reality. A place where things exist only in theory or suggestion rather than one in which they are actual and real.

Atheists and agnostics would be eager to jump on horses in hopes of finding support for their beliefs. They would no longer have to rely upon their think tank comprised of eenie, meenie, miny and moe in conjunction with the world renowned organization of E.I.E.I.O. A stampede in search of answers could occur.

Of all the things to wish for, and the list is endless, health would definitely be a very popular one. Health is defined as a state of physical, mental and social well-being. A place where disease and infirmity are absent. There is something missing from that definition. Physical, mental, and social well-being are key components to our overall health, but we must not overlook our spiritual well-being.

We are body, spirit, and soul. Spiritual well-being most definitely plays a part in our health. Disease and infirmity must be absent spiritually as well. The spiritual world is real. It is not just a theory or an imaginary place. One does not need to wish or jump aboard a horse going to make believe land to be spiritually healthy.

Spiritual well-being is when God's Spirit, the Holy Spirit dwells within us. "Do you not know that you are a temple of God and that the Spirit of God dwells in you?" (1 Corinthians 3:16) We don't have to wish for spiritual health. There is a path to good or improved health physically. There is a path to good health spiritually as well. That path begins by allowing God into your heart.

"A horse is a false hope for victory; Nor does it deliver anyone by its great strength." (Psalm 33:17) Dismissing spiritual well being as insignificant, or even imaginary, is unhealthy. Being in a state of spiritual wellness helps us feel more connected to a higher power as well as to those around us.

Being healthy includes all three components, body, mind and spirit. Spiritual health gives us a feeling of being connected, a sense of belonging. Being positive and optimistic are also examples of spiritual wellness. Being healthy, both physically and spiritually encourages us to practice self care because we feel healthy and want to remain healthy.

Being physically fit allows us to achieve things not possible by one who is not physically fit. The same is true spiritually. Overall fitness includes physical, emotional, social, intellectual as well as spiritual fitness. All are important for overall health. Spiritual health is too often neglected. Having a healthy relationship with God affects all other areas. It has a profound impact on all areas of our lives.

Health and strength do not come by wishful thinking. There is no magical horse to hop on that will take you to a place where you can be sprinkled with health dust. The best place to start is with the one who created us out of dust and breathed the breath of life into us. Searching anywhere else is really just wasting time fooling around or goofing off. You might even say that too many have saddled up and are just "horsing around." However you want to label it, it is not exhibiting mental health nor is it evidence of being healthy spiritually.

Hickory Dickory Dock

We have seen three mice that were blind, now let's take a look at one that seems to have a lot of energy, and a lot of friends. With each verse of this nursery rhyme the mouse is replaced.Verse two is a snake, verse three is a squirrel, verse four is a cat, five a monkey, and six an elephant. The elephant must have broken the clock because there seems to be no verse seven. When the clock struck the hour of the number of the verse each was a part of, down they went. Six o'clock must have been quitting time unless the clock was repaired and reinforced to support a climbing elephant.

What does it all mean? Some believe it refers to the son of an English General named Richard Cromwell, the son of Oliver Cromwell. He had a couple of nicknames "Tumbledown Dick" and "Hickory Dick" and only held office for one year. The clock striking one indicating after one year of service, he came down, or he was replaced.

There are various versions or ideas including one that claims hickory, dickory, dock derived from old Celtic numbers. Another claims it is a counting-out rhyme and yet another claims that the rhyme is based on the astronomical clock which had a hole in the door, just below the face so the resident cat could hunt mice. The things that all these claims have in common is that there was a clock, and that when the clock struck, things changed.

I wonder if any of those climbing the clock paid any attention to the hour approaching. You would think that had they observed previous attempts at climbing the clock, they would know what was coming. If they knew what was coming, surely they would have tried to avoid the inevitable. They would have made some kind of change, or take the necessary steps to avoid their fall. It seems as though they only paid attention to their personal ascension, ignoring everything else, only interested in reaching their goal. They paid no attention to time, no concern for anything other than what they wanted to do.

Does that sound familiar? I think it accurately describes far too many people today only interested in themselves and their personal agenda. So many trying to ascend their own clock, oblivious to anything else but themselves. No time for anyone or anything that hinders their path. No time for anything but themselves. Hickory, dickory, dock, pay attention to the clock.

Our time is precious. Not enough of it is spent with our spouse, or children, our entire family. The time we do spend needs to be quality time. Too many do not find or make time to spend with those we love and those who love us. Our schedules are so full we have come to accept the lack of time properly spent with loved ones as being normal or unavoidable. With so little time to divvy up, we justify spending little or none with the God who created us. We need to adjust our priorities and come to the realization of why we are here, how we got here and where we are going. When does the clock strike? Maybe we should take a closer look at time so things can be put in proper perspective.

We have all heard people say things like "time flies" or "I still have plenty of time" or "time to do this or that". Our perception and understanding is relevant to where we are in our lives. The dictionary describes time as the indefinite continued progress of existence and events in the past, present, and future regarded as a whole.

A young person looks at things as though he or she has plenty of time to live and experience life. That is true in most cases. An older person may think that time is running out. The older we get, the less time we have to live, and our days are numbered. The clock is indeed clicking, and as a song from the 70's says: "time keeps on slippin' slippin' slippin' into the future.

It is important to note here that time is the indefinite continued progress of existence. A 75 year old man may feel old, but how long is 75 years compared to forever? We continue to scurry along, busy running up the clock like the little mouse, or for some, like the monkey or elephant, paying little or no attention to the clock. The clock keeps on ticking and will do so indefinitely, for eternity. For the 75 year old man, there is plenty of future ahead and all of us should put that in perspective. Take a look at time from a perspective of forever and see if that doesn't change the way we look at, and run up the clock. Hickory, dickory, dock.

Row Row Row Your Boat

A boat being rowed gently down the stream depicts a tranquil and very peaceful setting. The boat probably left a hickory dock owned by Dick. Most likely a dock owned by Dick and Jane. We don't really know that for sure. All that we know for sure is that the boat was being propelled by oars, and it was not being done intensely or powerfully, but gently and merrily as if in a world without consideration of any possible problems, or unwelcome situations. An imaginary land, peaceful, perhaps a heavenly place.

A nursery rhyme and popular children's song explaining the importance of a positive attitude in life is the view of many. Some see this as a message to not quit and to keep going despite occasional or continual difficulties. Stay calm and keep rowing and calmers waters will come.

We all know that difficulties arise, obstacles suddenly appear, and that life is not always "smooth sailing", or more appropriately, smooth rowing. There are times of tranquility when things are calm with little or no disturbance, but often we find ourselves coming out of difficulty, entering a difficult stretch, or in the middle of one. The wind and waves do pick up and rowing requires more intensity.

What do we do in those times where we need a firmer grip on the oars and must put forth a greater effort to overcome? Do we run and hide in another boat as did Jonah, do we walk on water like Peter, or do we put the oars in the boat and drift to wherever the current takes us?

Society tells us to do whatever floats your boat. Anything is o.k. in order to achieve or accomplish whatever you want. The end justifies the means. You can make up the rules, or change them to accommodate your effort, all in the name of "progress".

The absence of God in our lives supports that philosophy and ideology. Man has most definitely drifted and the direction is away from God. The longer the drift continues, the further away from Him we get. Followers of Christ see that, and as we row our boat, we have a Helper. We do not always listen or pay attention to Him as we should, but He is always there for us. The boat stays afloat when the wind and waves pick up and it makes the journey down the river much easier. We do not live in an imaginary land. Our world is real, the Creator is real, life is real.

Merrily, merrily, life is but a dream is a reference to the belief that what we can dream we can make happen by believing in ourselves, by positive thinking. We can row our boat without consideration of problems or even future implications, by positive thinking. It is true that we must have confidence and determination to accomplish things and get things done, but is life like a dream? If a dream is a series of thoughts and images, or even sensations that are in a persons mind during sleep, than perhaps we can go merrily, merrily down the stream, carefree and problem free. That would not be descriptive of anyone I've ever met. Life is full of obstacles and barriers, hurdles and detours. How we react and respond to them depends upon what is in our hearts and minds. There is a big difference between God allowing something and God being a part of it and having His blessing! Life is not "but a dream", it can seem like it at times, but it is very much real. It has a purpose. We can dream about life being problem free, but then we wake up from that dream and have to deal with reality. We do not have to that alone.

How would you answer the question " Who's rowing your boat?" Are we rowing the boat? If we are, is it being done with God's guidance? Is He just a bystander ready to come to our assistance when we get into troubled waters or is He with us wherever we go providing continual guidance? Wouldn't it be nice if we had someone with us that could calm the wind and seas and help us through the storms that arise? We can, many of us do. Calming the storm is one of the miracles of Jesus reported in the Gospels. (Matthew 8:23-27), (Mark 4:35-41), (Luke 8:22-25) News Flash! The same Jesus that calmed the storms when He was with His followers, the disciples 2000 years ago, can calm the storms faced by His followers today.

Life is not just about keeping your head above water and remaining afloat. It makes a world of difference as to who is invited, and who is aboard the boat.

Jack and Jill

Most people are familiar with this nursery rhyme. The two, Jack and Jill went up a hill to get some water, he fell down and injured his head. Jill also fell down the hill, but she escaped injury. The remedy of the day for his head injury was vinegar and brown paper. Interesting how remedies and cures have changed over the years. The brown paper, back in the day, 18th and 19th centuries was made of rope, canvas, and other sacking, very coarse material. There have been many improvements made in many areas over time, yet in some ways we have not made progress, but in fact, gone backwards. The continued distancing ourselves from God is the most troublesome backward trend.

The relationship between Jack and Jill is uncertain. Many believe them to be brother and sister, others boyfriend and girlfriend, and some believe them to be two male friends. The latter belief stems from an early spelling of "Gill" for "Jill". The only thing we are sure of is that they had some kind of relationship, of which there are many. There are family relationships, friendships, acquaintanceships, and romantic relationships.

Too often overlooked, and the most important relationship of all, is our relationship with God.

There are key things that are essential in a good relationship. there must be trust, respect, love, attention and communication. Your closest and best relationships are because all of those characteristics exist in those relationships.

The difficulty for many in accepting that a relationship with God can exist is because one or more of those essential characteristics does not exist. One may not trust God because they think He is responsible for everything that happens, credit for the good and blame for the bad. They fail to realize that in the beginning everything was good and perfect. The game changer was when man brought sin into the world. The freedom of choosing that was given to man at creation paved the way for poor choices.

Love and respect cannot exist if there is no knowledge of God. If the perception of God is a transcendent power existing apart from the material universe and that He exists but is just "out there" somewhere, we cannot love Him, only fear Him. On the other hand, if we know Him as our Creator, our Savior, and have His Spirit living within us, we do love and respect Him. We do trust Him, pay attention to Him and communicate with Him. We do in fact have a relationship with Him.

Many believe that the Bible is a rulebook when in fact it teaches us that God wants a relationship with us. He pursues us through His Son. We were separated from Him through sin and reunited with Him through His incarnate Son.

The more quality time we spend with our friends, family, and loved ones the better the relationship. The same is true with our relationship with God. The more quality time we spend in prayer and in His Word, the better the communication, the stronger the trust, the love, and the respect.

A personal God can be related to as a person instead of some distant Absolute or impersonal force. God loves us and wants us to have a personal relationship with Him. Our relationships are many. We welcome the good ones, we embrace them and we need them. We need a relationship with God. There really is no life without Him, merely existence.

Jack and Jill went up the hill to fetch a pail of water. They both failed in their attempt. Do not fail in your attempt to find the Living Water, the Truth, a very real relationship with God. James 4:8 ESV says: "Draw near to God, and He will draw near to you."

Communication with God requires tuning into the right frequency. In other words, a quiet time void of interference and distractions. Communication does exist, it is not just a notional idea or something idealistic. It is real, having both existence and substance. I highly recommend tuning in.

A relationship means a connection. If there is no connection, there is no relationship. Claiming that there is not, or cannot be a relationship between us and God is the result of not being connected. Connecting is to become joined where there is communication.

The relationship between Jack and Jill is not really important. The establishment of a relationship with God is of utmost importance. A relationship that will last forever.

Jack Sprat

There certainly are a lot of nursery rhymes where this fellow named Jack is involved. He was very busy to say the least. He climbed bean stalks, and hills, and even jumped over candlesticks. Even though he fell down a hill and broke his crown, he was very nimble and quick. The term sprat was used to refer to short people back in the 16th century so, evidently, he wasn't very big. Since Jack is one of the most common names in the world, it would be safe to conclude that all these guys named Jack are not the same guy. The same Jack may have climbed a beanstalk and got thirsty and took his friend Jill to get some water. The same Jack may have become hungry after jumping over the likes of candlesticks and sought out a Christmas pie to satisfy that hunger. We just don't know for sure.

It is a high probability that Jack Horner and Jack Sprat are not the same fellow. They were both short, but they had different last names. Jack Sprat ate no fat and probably stayed away from sweet things like pies and cakes. There is a good possibility that the Christmas pie that little Jack Horner stuck his thumb into was a pie consisting of dried fruits and spices and may have been quite healthy. I guess we'll never know. We do know that Jack Sprat ate no fat and so, we will concentrate on that.

He must have been very disciplined and concerned for his health and well- being. His wife on the other hand, could eat no lean. Together they would lick the platter clean, one avoiding the fat the other avoiding the lean. Jack was old English. If we didn't know better we would think that his wife may be American. We know that is not true because this rhyme was long before America was on the scene. His wife's eating habits did resemble that of many American's. A diet of high fat content and little or no regard for the repercussions. The obesity rate is quite high in the USA because there is not enough attention paid to the negative impact obesity has on our health and wealth.

Jack Sprat's wife may have had a brother named Jimmy who shared his sister's disregard for good eating habits. I am referring to the Jimmy of "jimmy crack corn and I don't care." I really don't think that they were related, but they did share the same attitude of not caring, most likely about different issues.

The not caring attitude is popular about many things that should be given a greater amount of care, concern and concentration , but are not. We can chew the fat about many of those areas, but let's limit it to eating, what we feed upon and the responsibility we have in taking care of ourselves.

We all were encouraged to take care of ourselves by our parents when we were growing up and even into adulthood. Some listened, some did not. If we chose to do otherwise, directly or indirectly, we did, and we still do. Our habits have been determined by what we want, not limited to what we need. Our self serving desires control our actions. Our parents tried to put us on the right path, but they were just our parents, old fashioned, and putting a crimp on our freedom.

There was no directive, no official or authoritative instruction, or so it seemed, only suggestions by our parents that went in one ear and out the other. Determination to make our own decisions and not to be unduly interrupted in that process bordered on rebellion. That same attitude continues today.

The notion that there is no authoritative instruction regarding taking care of our bodies is completely wrong. Our bodies are God's workmanship, created by Him and expertly made. Reading in 1 Corinthians 6:19-20 we are told: "Or do you not know that your body is a temple of the Holy Spirit who is in you, whom you have from God…" That means you respect your body, be mindful of what you put into it. In Psalm 139 we read "we're fearfully and wonderfully made." We must respect our body, treat it well. We were created, redeemed by Christ, and can receive the indwelling of the Holy Spirit. Claiming those three things makes us a temple of God. A place where His Spirit resides.

When we invite people into our homes, we want everything to be in its proper place. We want the environment to be welcoming, and we want our guests to feel happy and accepted. The "red carpet" is rolled out for our guests. Certainly, there should be more emphasis put upon getting our house in order if the guest is our Creator. His Spirit dwells within those who's temple He has been welcomed into. Our bodies are that temple, and there needs to be tremendous importance put upon the maintenance of it. Red carpets are rolled out as privileged treatment of a distinguished visitor. The most distinguished of all, who is not just a visitor, but a permanent resident, demands our best. A diet of fat, or an unhealthy diet, and total disregard for our bodies is not our best.

As is the case with many nursery rhymes, Jack Sprat may have been the result of satire on a public figure. The dictionary describes "satire" as the use of humor, irony, exaggeration, or ridicule to criticize people's stupidity or vices. A vice is a moral failing or a bad habit.

We have bad habits and really are very stupid regarding proper maintenance of our bodies. A moral failure is an act or thought that is carried out when one knows that it should not be carried out. When God's Spirit dwells within us, we should pay attention to His guidance, rather than ignore Him.

The definition of a "fathead" is a stupid person. The fathead population is thriving and continues to wave the banner of ignorance and denial, deception and misconception.

To expect a Christian, a follower of Christ to be in tip top physical condition is not what I am saying. We need to be more mindful of temple maintenance and take the steps necessary, do what we can, and make a continued effort to be the best we can, physically, mentally, and spiritually. That's a fact Jack!

Mary Had A Little Lamb

This nursery rhyme is one of the most popular of all. It was first published back in 1830 and many believe it was actually inspired by an actual incident. A girl named Mary who had a pet lamb that followed her to school one day. The rhyme was also the first audio recorded by Thomas Edison who invented the phonograph in 1877.

If you recall, Little Bo Peep, lost her sheep, but Mary's little lamb was so attached to her that it followed her around. Some draw parallels between Mary the mother of Jesus and Mary in the rhyme. The rhyme is about Mary loving the lamb and the lamb loving Mary. Jesus is referred to in scripture as the Lamb of God. Maybe we should take a closer look at that.

It is important to understand that the significance of the Lamb as pointed out in both the old and new testaments of the Bible. The use of a lamb for sacrifice was something that the Jewish people were accustomed to when worshipping God. Using animal sacrifices was a way for God's people to temporarily atone for their sins. Since there is a penalty for sin, sacrifices were a way to temporarily atone, or make amends for those sins. They were a reparation for an offense.

Jesus, referred to as the Lamb of God by John the Baptist, was the ultimate sacrificial lamb when He died for our sins on the cross. He rose again, payment was made, and He is alive today. John the Baptist used the expression "Lamb of God" as a reference to the ultimate sacrifice of Jesus. Look at John 1:29; "Behold the Lamb of God who takes away the sin of the world." Another such reference appears in John 1:36; "And looking upon Jesus as He walked, he saith, Behold the Lamb of God."

Keep in mind that these references were made before Jesus died on the cross. They also appear in the old testament of the Bible. A lamb was offered as daily sacrifices (Leviticus 14:12-21) A lamb was used for sacrifice during Passover (Exodus 12:1-36) The 53rd chapter of Isaiah tells of a lamb being led to slaughter, a reference to Jesus, the sacrificial Lamb of God.

It is important to note hear how the entire Bible, both old and new testaments together show God's plan for humanity from beginning to end. Together they show who God is and what he is like.

Mary had a little lamb and everywhere that Mary went, the lamb was sure to go. We need to have the Spirit of God dwelling within us be with us wherever we may go. How great are any sacrifices we may make in order to maintain a great relationship with Him? They do not compare to the ultimate sacrifice that was made for us by the Lamb of God.

Mary's little lamb had fleece as white as snow. Check out another reference from the book of Isaiah. Chapter 1 verse 18 says; "Though your sins are as scarlet, They will be white as snow; Though they are red like crimson, They will be like wool". The Lamb of God took upon the sins of mankind as if to absorb all the color. The scarlet of sin has been changed to white as snow. That transformation occurs when we are born again. White as snow implies purity, a freedom from adulteration or contamination.

The follower of Christ is like a sheep who needs a shepherd. We need help in trying to avoid contamination, there certainly is plenty of that in the world today. Our help comes from the Helper, God's Holy Spirit.

Just as Mary had a close relationship with her little lamb, we need a close relationship with the Lamb of God. Her little lamb followed her to school one day. We need the Lamb of God in our lives every single day and need to follow Him.

There are 43 Bible verses about God as Shepherd, I will reference only a couple. Psalm 95:7 reads; "For He is our God, and we are the people of His pasture and the sheep of His hand…." He is the Good Shepherd (John 10:11). We are His flock.

When Mary went to school one day, the little lamb followed her and was eventually turned out. The little lamb lingered near because he loved Mary. How many times has Jesus been turned down, turned out, rejected and ignored? Jesus is near because He loves us. He waits with outstretched arms, welcoming us because of that love.

Do you think Mary was embarrassed by the little lamb's presence? He loved her so much that he followed her around wanting to be with her and to be a part of her life. She could have done as the teacher and sent the lamb away. The teacher sent the little lamb away because it was a distraction and against the rules. The lamb waited patiently until Mary appeared.

As a result of the lamb's patience and Mary not rejecting him, both enjoyed happiness and joy and maintained a relationship anchored by love. The lesson here is obvious. Jesus is constantly rejected because welcoming Him may create a fear of becoming a distraction or seen as going against the norm. Some man made rule may be violated. A rule made up by rule makers still in the dark or driven by personal agendas. There is a pushing away rather than a pulling towards. The source of love and joy is turned away. Heartbreak results rather than happiness, rejection is chosen over regeneration. Mary embraced the little lamb, we need to embrace the Lamb of God and follow Him home one day.

Goosey Goosey Gander

This particular nursery rhyme isn't as well know as some, but was particularly popular in the 16th century. The second line asks the question "where shall I wander." It is believed by many that this refers to itinerant priests who traveled around seeking hiding places to avoid persecution from the Protestants who were totally against the Catholic religion. This was happening during the time of Henry VII and later during the time of Oliver Cromwell. There is also the belief that there was a wandering clergy because they had no benefice or had deserted the church.

Persecution for religious beliefs has been going on for centuries. Hostility and ill treatment of those having an opposing view or belief is nothing new. Christians, or followers of Christ, have been persecuted since the time of Jesus. He was persecuted and crucified, fulfilling many Biblical prophecies that had been written hundreds of years beforehand.

Freedom of worship and religious freedom protects people's right to speak and act, and to live according to their beliefs. What we know today as freedom, did not exist long ago, and still doesn't exist in some portions of the world today. It may seem hard to believe by some, because we have taken it for granted.

A period known as the Great Persecution, during the Roman Empire around the year 303 saw edicts issued which rescinded Christian's legal rights. Those edicts demanded compliance to traditional religious practices. Persecution for faith and non traditional religious activities was very prevalent throughout our history. Non compliance had its repercussions. Priests were wandering to avoid persecution from the Protestants, as we see when we take a gander at this nursery rhyme. To what extent have we gone or will we go to avoid persecution as a Christian?

Paul the Apostle, commonly known as St Paul and also known by his Hebrew name Saul of Tarsus taught the gospel of Christ in the first century, and was on both sides of persecution. He persecuted the Church and was later persecuted himself, beheaded, because of his faith.

The biblical accounts of Paul persecuting the church are in the books of Galations (1:13) and in Acts (8:1). He saw Jewish Christians as obstacles to his advancement in Judaism, the Jewish system comprised of religious, cultural and legal traditions of the Jewish people. What a change, from persecuting to persecuted. What happened?

We can get clarity by looking at the 9th chapter of the book of Acts. The conversion of Paul was an event that led him to stop persecuting the early Christians and become a follower of Jesus. This a familiar account by most Christians and is known as The Damascus Road, or what happened to Paul on his way to Damascus. Paul saw a bright light and fell to the ground, "and heard a voice saying to him, Saul, Saul, why are you persecuting Me?" And he said "Who are you Lord?" And He said, I am Jesus whom you are persecuting." (9:4-5)

Paul was converted and went on to write letters to many churches and is credited with the authorship of many books in the New Testament. There is little doubt that he, more than any other individual, was responsible for the spread of Christianity throughout the vast Roman Empire.

His writings help to explain and encourage believers. They help in grasping an understanding of the Christian walk. They are a wonderful source of Paul's life and of his thought. He is passionate about bringing the message of the crucified Messiah to all, city by city.

Wandering around aimlessly like geese, or like priests ,or like anyone, who seek refuge where ever they can, will find that that refuge is only temporary. They will have to move on, continuing to wander because their refuge, their being safe or sheltered from pursuit, danger or trouble will not last forever.

It is a matter of temporary versus eternal. We find refuge in whatever we can, wandering and roaming around, going from one place to another without a plan or definite purpose. Life does have a purpose. What are the most important things in your life? Do we try to rid any obstacles in our way of building our shelter of refuge? We don't want to wander aimlessly from place to place so we go to great lengths to fortify our shelter. We become defensive and close minded leading to issuing our own edicts rejecting anything that is contrary to our own definition of acceptable, and demanding compliance to our man made rules which seem to drift further and further away from those established by our Creator. Stop wandering around and find your own "Road to Damascus." Seek and you will find.

Those who have found that road, have found salvation and know Truth and peace are not without persecution. There remains persecution from those that do not agree with the teachings of the Gospels. There are those who do not believe and there are those who go through a reoccurring affliction of "gospel amnesia," a term that I have heard a few times and experienced too many times.

Stop wandering aimlessly, find purpose and peace. The peace of God, which surpasses all comprehension, transcends all understanding will indeed guard our hearts and minds for those who are in Christ. (Philippians 4:6-7).

Human nature makes us inclined to take control of our lives. When we do that, we end up pushing out the one that gave us life in the first place. Wandering around aimlessly, roaming from place to place, are we like those that seek refuge, looking for a place of safety? Do we constantly meander about seeking a place that is sheltered from danger and trouble? If you persist and just continue to wander, you'll likely miss the roll call up yonder.

Baa, Baa, Black Sheep

A nursery rhyme going way back with differing opinions over the years as to its real meaning. The earliest version goes back to 1731 and is widely regarded as referring to complaints against taxes levied on the buying and selling of wool. There was concern raised over its political correctness, but those concerns have been widely dispelled. That concern was about the black sheep being a reference to slaves.

Taking a closer look at what is meant by "black sheep" may help in gaining clarity here. We understand the meaning of the black sheep of the family as meaning the oddball, or the worst member of the family. We associate words like outcast, reject, or bad apple to black sheep. Just like the last person chosen in a pick up game, the black sheep has been associated with the least desired.

Taxation is not generally welcome with open arms and is viewed as negative or a last resort, unwelcome and unwanted. The black sheep was seen in the same way. The wool from a black sheep was less desirable because of the difficulty it presented in the dyeing process. A black sheep was rare and was viewed as an oddball. Taxes were not welcome, black sheep were not welcome. It was not uncommon where black sheep were unceremoniously culled, removed because they were considered of little or no use. Sometimes extreme measures are taken to remove and eradicate things that are considered of little use or of little value.

A voice that proclaims anything that is different, or not in complete agreement with the close-knit herd is considered problematic, an outcast, an oddball, a black sheep. Efforts are often put into action to remove the black sheep from the herd.

The black sheep becomes isolated and is separated from the herd. He is set apart from them and considered a threat to them. The voice of truth and of Godliness is seen by many in the same way. It is becoming less and less welcome to the ears of the herd. That voice is seen as coming from an outcast, an oddball and one of insignificance. The words are like blah, blah, blah black sheep and fall upon deaf ears.

The word sanctify means to be set apart, set apart from all else and dedicated to God. We must be aware of the wolves in sheep's clothing and, "Sanctify them in the truth." (John 17:17) We must also be aware of the ongoing efforts to still that voice. We have seen the trend for years of distancing from God and His Word. It is evident in values, in morals, and fundamental principles, all of which are based upon the foundation set by God. That trend of distancing is the continual effort of pulling the wool over our eyes. The wool of the black sheep proclaiming the truth is of no use in that effort. It is too difficult to work with. It cannot be altered or dyed. The color of the truth cannot be changed, it is natural, not made or caused by mankind. It is unchangeable regardless of any efforts made to alter it. That includes the efforts of the many wolves in sheep's clothing.

This Little Piggy

This nursery rhyme is quite old, from the 1700's. The rhyme continued to appear since that time with moderate variations. The meaning may surprise you. It is believed the meaning was about pigs going to market, not to buy things, but to be slaughtered for food. Each line of this nursery rhyme tells of the condition, or status of each little piggy as to the readiness for going to market. Staying home meant not ready for market. Having roast beef alludes to fattening up to be in the right condition to go. Just before going to market pigs are not fed in order to facilitate the process, perhaps alluding to the little piggy having none. Going home meant not sold and returning home alive and squealing out of joy for avoiding further steps leading to the dinner table.

I like the less dark interpretation of this nursery rhyme. The one being about this little family of five, each going about their business, and contributing whatever they could to the well being of pig land. Reciting the lines of this nursery rhyme to a child while counting their toes and tickling the child as you say "wee wee wee all the way home", paints a much better picture for me then that of a slaughterhouse. You can decide for yourself the version you prefer.

I have always viewed this nursery rhyme as portraying a feeling of pleasure and contentment as opposed to death and slaughter and will proceed by taking that path. The path of going to the market, not going to market.

I took a speech class when I was in college and one assignment was to make a speech delivering the lines of a nursery rhyme. I just happened to choose this one. I added a bit of explanation for each piggy's actions showing how they all contributed and were an important part of their family.

The presentation was unique in that it was done from a chair atop a desk. I put a chair on the top of the thick wooden desk in the front of the classroom. I climbed up, took the shoe and sock off of my left foot then proceeded with my "speech." It was a huge success and everyone was smiling. The result would have been much different had I used the darker interpretation. The feeling of togetherness, acceptance, and worth is definitely much better than a feeling of "who's next."

The group of five was happy and content. They each had their strengths and weaknesses and their own roles in contributing to the efficiency and effectiveness of their lives. Working together, each having a function or part to perform in a particular operation or process results in a smoother process and a better result.

As a business owner I knew of the importance of each one doing their part and contributing. All parts must work together. An engine requires many parts to perform. Moving forward is slowed down or stopped when all are not working together. A reliance and dependence develops amongst the group. Each one attends to one's obligation, each one carries one's share of the burden or one holds up his or her end. You do what you have promised to do or what you are expected to do.

In this group of five little piggies, one may go to the market for groceries. Another may stay home and cook or clean. One may have some roast beef because he worked late and missed dinner while another didn't have any because he was vegetarian. As for the last one, I think he was anxious to be on his way home and was yelling yes, yes, yes all the way home. He was obviously speaking in French so maybe this originated in France, or maybe he was bilingual.

It is also obvious that my account of their actions is silly. The point is that we all are important and play a significant role in determining the success and course along which we go. That is exactly what Paul was referring to in 1 Corinthians 12 when he speaks of unity and diversity in one body. He used the human body as an analogy for the unity of the church, the unity of the Church In Christ.

Just as a body, though it is one body, has many parts, they all form one body. By using this illustration we see that every part is essential to a functioning body. It is important to understand that unity is an absolute necessity for the church. Some lack consideration of others and are mainly concerned for personal profit or pleasure. That is the definition of "selfish."

Many are not happy with their role(s) or discontent with their gifts and want a role or gift they have not been given. They are then susceptible to counterfeit gifts and have opened a door where encouragement of self- centeredness comes in.

The categories of ministries, callings, and giftedness are illegitimate unless directed by God. Self-centeredness breaks up the unity thereby inviting adulteration and contamination.

The body functions with togetherness of parts. There is proximity to another, there is companionship where close attention is apparent. Paul uses the human body as an analogy for the unity of the church.(1 Corinthians 12:12) All must work together. When the door to selfishness is opened only slightly, the companionship and attention shifts from God to man. That door needs to be closed. We need to be of the same mind, maintaining the same love, united in spirit, intent on one purpose as Paul so appropriately wrote (Philippians 2:2).

Togetherness, same mind, united in spirit, one purpose. The purpose of glorifying God while enjoying life, not just tolerating it and trying to live it solely under self control. Whether a party of five, as with the five little piggies, or a worldwide party of millions, we need to do what it takes to live the abundant life and spread the good news. We can do that by paying more attention to the blueprint for success outlined in the Bible. We all are important and must work together to be effective disciples, not drawing attention to ourselves, but drawing attention to God.

There Was An Old Woman Who Lived In A Shoe

This Mother Goose tale paints a picture of a woman who was at the point of not knowing what to do. Many believe that living in a shoe is a metaphor for living in poverty. Some think that the shoe was left by a giant who kidnapped the woman's husband. The shoe was later made into a place to live by some of her many children. There are some who think that the theme of this nursery rhyme is survival and a mother's love.

One thing we can be sure of is that the woman was old, the nursery rhyme is old, and she was so overwhelmed by her circumstances that she did not know what to do. Sound familiar? We have all been there. A feeling of having too many irons in the fire, or too much on our plates has become commonplace. It is not unusual to feel uncertain as to where to go or what to do.

We have all found ourselves in the midst of stormy whether or turbulent waters and our reaction to it determines our direction. Let me repeat, our direction has a destination. The old woman did not know what to do to change her situation, but she did not give up. A follower of Christ may face a situation where there is uncertainty and may not know what to do. It may be a result of memory lapses, or making bad choices. One might choose pause or neglect, maybe disregarding or perhaps ignoring and overlooking the proper path. Challenges are many and they come often. Being properly equipped to face those challenges is critical in getting through them.

The book of Job tells us of the many hurdles or obstacles encountered by the man Job. Pain and suffering are a part of our human experience. The book of Job shows us that when we go through difficult, discouraging and even traumatic experiences, we must trust God. We must be both trusting and patient as we await resolutions to our problems. Job lost his children, his health and his property. Some people seemingly lose their mind if the mail is not delivered on time.

What is the message here? We honor God when our troubles are over by thanking Him and giving Him praise. What we need to understand is that we honor God by staying committed to Him during those troubles. When we have so many children we don't know what to do, or when we face difficult circumstances in various ways, we need to realize we are not alone.

Faith is defined as complete trust or confidence in someone or something. If we do not have complete trust in God the door is left open for doubt to creep in. If it is not complete trust, it is incomplete trust. The definition of incomplete is not having the necessary or appropriate parts.

Complete trust and faith includes God and the knowledge that He has everything under control. We need to understand that wherever we may find ourselves, God will never desert us nor forsake us. (Heb 13:5) Take a look at what 2nd Timothy 1:7 says: "For God has not given us a spirit of fear, but of power and love and a sound mind." A sound mind exhibits self control and self discipline, not fear and panic.

I want to share a couple of quotes from a man named Oswald Chambers. He was an early twentieth century Scottish Baptist evangelist and teacher. "We have to pray with our eyes on God, not on the difficulties." It could not have been said any better, it is so true. He is also quoted as saying: "Your mind is the greatest gift God has given you, and it ought to be devoted entirely to Him."

The old woman in the shoe, with her hands full, did not know what to do. Followers of Christ, with hearts and minds full, do know what to do. The fullness of His indwelling Spirit makes it much easier to handle a full plate.

My Little Old Man

Little is known about this nursery rhyme. The place of origin and the history of this lessor known nursery rhyme seems to be a mystery. Many seem to parody the leaders and politics of their time. Though the history seems unknown, the topic is very well known. The problems regarding money and the noise and disruption it creates for far too many people. I will share the lyrics because most have not heard of it before.

> "My little old man and I fell out,
> I'll tell you what it was all about
> I had money and he had none
> And that's the way the noise begun"

Let me begin by quoting a well known verse from the Bible. 1 Timothy 6:10 states "For the love of money is a root of all sorts of evil, and some by longing for it have wandered away from the faith and pierced themselves with many griefs." Money itself is not evil, but the love of money, as scripture says, is a root for all sorts of evil. Problems surface, disagreement occurs, and the noise begins as the root is fed because of a lack of understanding.

Luke 12:15 helps put this in perspective: "Then He (Jesus) said to them, "Beware, and be on your guard against every form of greed; for not even when one has an abundance does his life consist of his possessions. The "worth" of a person is not measured in dollars. Possessions do not determine the real value of life.

Having a proper desire for things we need in our lives is very normal and it is a motivation to work in order to provide for ourselves. Coveting and longing for things we don't have can be a result of an insatiable desire, a desire that is impossible to satisfy.

Each person needs to follow their own convictions regarding stewardship, being mindful of the fact that everything belongs to our Creator anyway. We need to manage and utilize all resources that God provides us with, for His glory, and for the betterment of His creation. Money is just one thing. Everything that God allows us to have, or that He brings into our lives should be managed in a way that brings honor to Him.

We are quick to get noisy when what is received, or what is dispersed, is not exactly as we each think is appropriate. When the handling of money does not agree with each individuals own method, style, or manner, sounds begin and noise is heard. Those sounds are usually loud or unpleasant and cause disturbance. The noise has begun. Proper stewardship is important because it promotes a culture of both transparency and accountability. Noise is minimized, and the characteristics of responsibility and accountability are on full display. Characteristics that are aligned with the expectations of our Creator.

There is the element of common sense as well. The problem with that, as has been mentioned many times, is that common sense isn't that common. We must be sensible and take a course of action that is in accordance with wisdom and prudence. Having knowledge is not the same as having wisdom. We can have knowledge of facts and truths and even principles. Wisdom is the ability to apply that knowledge to the way our lives are led.

The Bible tells us that "The fear of the Lord is the beginning of wisdom" (Psalm 111:10) and "Do not be wise in your own eyes; Fear the Lord and turn away from evil" (Proverbs 3:7) In matters regarding money, we must use wisdom. The wisdom that is revealed by our actions must be determined by our knowledge of Biblical truths and principles not merely what is seen by our own eyes.

The Bible also tells us that we cannot serve God and wealth (Luke 16:13). Devotion to God and devotion to money are not compatible. Many of the Pharisees believed they were. If you recall, the Pharisees were an ancient Jewish sect who strictly observed the traditional and written law. They regarded themselves as having superior sanctity, or having a quality of being more saintly.

The same belief is held today that devotion to God and devotion to money are compatible. In far too many cases, devotion to money is far more important than devotion to God. When our eyes become improperly fixed we have become wise in our own eyes, which is not true wisdom.

My Little Old Man

There was noise between the old man and the woman in this rhyme. There will be noise and unwanted sound, when we do not properly apply our knowledge of scripture. We must be wise in His eyes.

Little Miss Muffet

A very popular nursery rhyme that was first recorded back in 1805. As is the case with many nursery rhymes the origin is unclear and there are a variety of ideas intended to provide explanations. As a child, I was especially interested in finding an explanation of what a tuffet was, and what exactly are curds and whey? A tuffet is a tuft, a clump of something, or a low seat. Perhaps a rounded clump of grass making a comfortable seat. I'm still not sure about curds and whey. It was some kind of cheese product from back in the day.

It was first recorded in 1805, but there are many who believe its origin was in the 1600's and Miss Muffet was actually the daughter of Dr Thomas Muffet an English physician and entomologist who may have had a collection of spiders.

Some things are unclear. What is very clear is that when a spider sat down beside her, Miss Muffet was scared away. She was afraid and ran away. There was an unpleasant feeling which was triggered by the perception of danger. There are many things that trigger the same response in some. A fear or phobia of various things. She may have had a fear of spiders known as arachnophobia.

There are many phobias, a fear of something that causes one to want to avoid it. It is believed that there are more than six million people in the United States with some type of phobia. A phobia may worsen if not treated, even to the extent where life is seriously impacted. Several areas in a persons life could be strongly affected. Physical health problems, problems with friends or family, even failure in school, just to mention a few.

There are a surprisingly large number of phobias. Fear of public speaking is the number one phobia in America. Others include clowns, ghosts, and zombies. There is a fear of flying, fear of heights, fear of enclosed spaces. A fear of snakes, of dogs, of insects, and of storms. The list goes on and on. As I mentioned, it is believed that America's number one phobia is the fear of public speaking. I am not going to challenge that claim but I think there is a phobia that is much bigger than we think. That is "alethophobia", a fear or dislike of the truth. I am not making this up. Fearing and denying the truth is very much a reality.

Little Miss Muffet was scared away by something that triggered her feeling of danger, a spider. Does one who fears the truth become scared and flee when they are confronted with the truth? There are many who do. We should not be afraid of the truth, we should embrace it. We should not flee from it, but run to it.

When Jesus was speaking to the Jews who believed Him, believed He was the Son of God, and persevered or continued in "My word" (studying, and learning from scripture) and holds fast, obeys and practices His teaching, then: "you will know the truth, and the truth will make you free". (John 8:32) The truth is more than the fact of Him being the Messiah and the Son of God, it is also about the truth of His teaching that an obedient follower will know divine truth and freedom from sin.

Jesus said: "I am the way, and the truth, and the life; no one comes to the Father but through Me'.(John 14;6) He is the truth of God and the way to God. Life, eternally is through salvation, deliverance from sin and its consequences brought about by faith in Christ.

Does that truth create fear and make some flee and run away from the truth? Would some flee if they were sitting on their tuffet and someone put a Bible beside them? The Bible is the Word of God showing God's plan for humanity, it is Divine Revelation, a collection of 66 documents inspired by God. Hardly anything to fear.

It should be pointed out that at the time when Jesus was doing His teaching, those listening did not have the advantage of reading the New Testament, the second part of the Christian biblical canon. We do have that advantage and can see the Bible in its entirety, seeing how it is Divine Revelation. To quote one of my favorite Bible "experts" Perry Stone: "the old testament is the new testament concealed, the new testament is the old testament revealed". The plan from beginning to end.

Even with the advantage of having and studying both the old and the new testaments, rejection, denial, and fear of the truth is very prevalent. Opposition hides the truth, to many the truth triggers a feeling of danger. Danger that truth will upset the apple cart and a reset would be needed. A reset that would involve an adjustment, a repair, or some kind of change.

Opposition does not want that type of change, and will avoid reset at all costs. Apple carts are full and they are numerous. The abundance of apples on the carts come from the same tree that Adam and Eve ate from. We know how that worked out. We know the answer if we were to ask them: "How you like them apples?" Avoid them apples, feed on the Truth. enjoy the fruits of the Spirit!

Tweedledee And Tweedledum

These two characters are fictional characters in an English nursery rhyme. They were characters satirizing disagreements as far back as 1700. They were used to criticize and expose peoples stupidity and vices. They appear in a letter in 1921 to characterize the conflict between Sigmund Freud and Carl Gustav Jung and again in the 1951 version of Alice in Wonderland. They have appeared in various writings and articles over the years. Helen Keller said of democracy that we choose between two autocrats, we choose between Tweedledum and Tweedledee.

A more modern version would be dumb and dumber. A movie was made not long ago with that title. It was about two characters sharing a lack of intellectual acuity where every day was a no brainer. There was an article written in a Christian magazine about how Biblical illiteracy is killing our Nation. The words Dumb and Dumber were in the title.

The movie referred to came out more than 25 years ago and the article over 5 years ago. Regarding Biblical principles and fundamental truths, the direction we have gone since then has been steadily downward. A movement from a higher level or place to a lower level or place. The foundation was crumbling as we sat back watching while depending on dumb and dumber to take care of things.

Dumb and dumber is not a direct reflection on just two people as in the movie, but on all those responsible for the erosion and decline of values. It is a description of the overall attitude and reaction to the downward trend. It is a reflection of the acceptance and endorsement of that movement away from the God and His Word. The Bible has had a tremendous impact on America, and still does. As its importance is diminished, our morals and values will also be diminished.

Those values are being uprooted and pulled out of their foundation. A foundation made up of rich soil providing the key to health and vitality. They are steadily being removed from the underlying support of life giving and life enriching principles.

The uprooted values are being replaced under the guise of progress and the replacement is like weeds invading a beautiful garden. A weed is a plant growing wild. It grows where it is not wanted and is in competition with cultivated plants. Its tendency is to overgrow and choke out more desirable plants.

The weeds are invasive and work their way inside boundaries. Boundaries made to provide protection and make safe that which is inside those boundaries. We take action to protect our gardens from the invasions of that which will take over and choke out our cultivated plants. Cultivation is nurturing and helping things grow. We need to take action and prevent the invasion of belief systems that are trying to choke out the principles and tenets laid out by our Creator. Weed out the bad and cultivate the good.

We have seen a continued movement from Tweedledee and Tweedledum to Dumb and Dumber. Continued movement in the same direction, sliding down the slippery slope, could very possibly result in the necessity of a more appropriately named duo. The movement would then be from Tweedledee and Tweedledum to Dumb and Dumber to Nincompoop and More Nincompoop. That movement must be prevented. We do not want to be around an excess of Nincompoop, we need to stop its spread.

Stay within the boundaries and parameters of our Biblical foundation and do not be swayed by the invasion of belief systems that are contrived, or deliberately created rather than arising naturally. That which was created by God is far superior than anything man is capable of creating. There is no substitute. One is pure, one is impure. One is right and one is wrong. One is unadulterated, one is not. Get rid of the weeds in your garden and blossom like our Creator wants you to. Don't be a nincompoop.

It's Raining It's Pouring

This is an English nursery rhyme and children's song. The words tell us about an old man who went to bed while it was pouring outside, bumped his head on the way to bed, fell asleep, was snoring, and did not get up in the morning.

There is uncertainty as to whether the old man ever woke up. Many have offered their opinion, but that question remains unanswered. There is also uncertainty if this old man was the husband of the old lady that lived in a shoe. Perhaps he was the same old man that played knick knack paddy whack and gave his dog a bone. We just don't know for sure. We can be sure that he fell asleep and was snoring.

Sleep is a necessity, it plays an important role in our physical health. We all know that. We also have realized that it accounts for about one third of our lives. We seem to fall asleep easier when it is raining, not necessarily when it is pouring like in the case of the old man.

There are various reasons and conditions that cause us to get sleepy. Being tired and worn out, being board, the soothing sound of a gentle rain, or simply being very comfortable are all situations that may help us fall asleep.

A pouring rain is not usually conducive to sleeping conditions, maybe the bump on the head had something to do with it. Being very comfortable is usually a requirement to falling asleep. He was an old man and probably fell asleep quite easily.

Falling asleep at the wrong time can result in unfavorable circumstances as we all know too well. Falling asleep in a meeting would be embarrassing, especially if it was accompanied by snoring. Falling asleep at the wheel of a moving vehicle would most certainly have much worse results.

Getting too comfortable can put us into a slumber and even into a deeper spiritual sleep. We can become so comfortable that we develop spiritual lethargy and apathy. Many need to awaken from that sleep as described by Paul in Romans 13:11. There are repercussions from that as well. We can become complacent and indifferent when we should be alert. We should not live like the sleeping who are in the dark, but like the enlightened children of God. Paul says in 1 Thessalonians 5:6: "so then let us not sleep as others do, but let us be alert and sober". We should not sleep in spiritual indifference. When we sleep we cease paying attention. That is true both physically and spiritually.

We need to see a raised awareness of the slumber that results when we get too comfortable. We need to raise our level of attention to what is going on both around us and inside of us. There is a saying to " let sleeping dogs lie." The meaning is to ignore a problem because, if dealt with, would cause an even more difficult situation. To let spiritual sleeping dogs lie results in a stunting of spiritual growth and dormancy, passiveness, sluggishness, apathy and insensibility. Those are not qualities of followers of Christ and are not characteristics of disciples or disciple makers.

We have become so wired to seek comfort at any cost. We seek bigger, faster, and easier, while pursuing physical ease and complete freedom from any pain or constraint. The freedom from pain and constraint makes us comfortable. We get comfortable, we go to sleep. It's raining, it's pouring and too many are snoring. We should be quick to notice things that may be unusual or are potentially dangerous. We need to be alert not asleep. It is time to wake up, be aware and be alert.

Pop Goes The Weasel

There is also much debate with this nursery rhyme as to its meaning and origin. There is, however, much agreement about it being a source of a dance tune. The tune remained the same but the words and meanings changed. There are variations from political references, to pawns as a chess piece or pawn as in collateral when borrowing money, to a small mammal, the weasel, just to mention a few. In each version the phrase, "pop goes the weasel" was present.

We do know that weasels pop their heads up out of their burrows when curious or disturbed. Changing the words and references from one variation to another is simply an attempt to draw attention to a variety of concerns. A disturbed weasel could signify an interference with normal arrangements or interference with the functioning of something.

There may also be significance by the use of a weasel here as opposed to another animal that may be drawn out of hiding or from a place not seen. The weasel is a small, carnivorous, slender mammal that is an active hunter. They are also very cunning.

Pop Goes The Weasel

The phrase "he weaseled his way," or "they weaseled out of" is used to mean great skill was used in the achieving one's ends by the use of deceit or evasion. A deceitful or treacherous person is often referred to as a " weasel." A criminal could weasel his way out of a guilty verdict. A product or a philosophy could be promoted via a cunning and deceit filled presentation. By concealing or misrepresenting the truth, an interference with normal arrangements and an interference with natural and intended functions are disrupted. Natural functions are based on an inherent, a permanent and essential sense of right and wrong. Man is weaseling his way from that definition to a self proclaimed definition of right and wrong.

The weasel will stay in his burrow until that redefining campaign is interrupted. When Christian voices arise, so do the weasels. Many of those Christian voices are silent as they remain sequestered in their borrows not wanting to be disturbed, comfortable in being isolated and hidden. They remain hunkered down in their foxholes, afraid or unwilling to go to battle against the opposition.

Those voices need to be heard, soldiers need to go to battle, putting on the full armor of God (Ephesians 6:11). We must be equipped to combat and thwart the adversary. Remaining silent and secluded within our own comfort zones does not help in the spreading of the truth. We must be active, an instrument to be used in the moving of God's Spirit. Active in promoting and supporting, actively encouraging the progress of His Spirit. We do not aid in that effort by inactivity. The weaseling out of the truth by our adversary continues, there is much activity. We must be very active to combat it.

The dove represents peace, love, renewal of life and a spirit messenger. It is a symbol of eternal peace and a symbol of the Holy Spirit. (Matt 3:16 Mark 1:10 Luke 3:22 John 1:32) A dove or a weasel, truth or untruth, natural or unnatural? The choice should be quite easy.

As our voices increase, the more activity will be shown by weasels appearing all over the place. That increased activity has been evident for many years. A good reason for more of the unheard Christian voices to be heard. An increased popping up of weasels requires an uproar, an increased popping up of voices of truth. The weasels will continue to pop, the competing voices will try to make themselves heard. We must make sure that our voices are heard. They may pop, we must explode. We must burst and break apart the untruth and deceit, spilling and exposing the corrupt, flawed and treacherous message that continues to be promoted by deceitful weasels. Truth, not untruth, it's time to pop up, step up and rise to the occasion.

A Tisket A Tasket

An American original dating back to 1879 having no specific meaning. It consists of word play made up to go with a popular singing game for kids. The catchy tune is used in jazz and led to a hit song back in 1938. Variations do exist but what they have in common is variations of basket color and the dropping of something then placed into the basket or into a pocket. It was a children's rhyming game sung while dancing around a circle.

Since there is no specific meaning, maybe we can attribute our own. Running around in circles is descriptive of a lot of people in their indecision of where to go, how to go or even whether they should go or not. Dropping something, whether intentional or not, is certainly very common. Picking something up and putting in a basket or a pocket is certainly not unusual. There is quite a variety of baskets and they aren't all green and yellow, there is a lot of diversity.

I don't want to go around in circles trying to come up with a meaning so I will limit my scrutiny to the basket, a container used to hold or carry things. They could be used for harvesting, transporting, or for both utilitarian and aesthetic purposes. Could they be used either knowingly or unknowingly in a negative way? The answer to that is a definite yes.

We live in a society where acquiring things is encouraged and is seen as a measuring stick of accomplishment and success. The one with the most toys wins. The bigger and more, the better. The amount of things in our basket is one thing, but to many the glitter and shine of those things is of greater importance. So, what's the problem?

We have a purpose to glorify God and to make disciples of others. (Matthew 28:19) We are to let our light shine before men. (Matthew 5:16) When we fill our baskets full of glitter, bling and so many shiny things, we have created such a glare that seeing anything is very difficult. No one can see our light because we blind them by our own addiction to acquire things.

If we are the light of the world we must let our light shine. Matthew 5:14-16 tells us that our light cannot be hidden and that no one lights a lamp and puts it under a basket. Many are guilty of doing just that. The basket can be used in such a way as to be rendered useless in our efforts to let our light shine and be instrumental in enlightening others. Both we and the basket are useless under those conditions. We have then become a basket case.

Rather than run around in circles singing a tisket a tasket and trying to fill our basket, we should be living and singing "this little light of mine, I'm gonna let it shine..........hide it under a bushel No"

I Had A Little Nut Tree

This rhyme has been around for a long time, since 1797. Some believe it had its origin as far back as 1506. There are historical figures attributed to both times so the debate continues. Nutmeg refers to the spices traded between England and the Far East. The pear is reference to the agricultural produce of England. The tree in this nursery rhyme seems to only bear silver nutmeg and a golden pear. It is a reference to the commodities highly sought after and their importance to trade.

No need to consult an arborist or a tree surgeon or any professional who studies trees to know that a tree only bearing silver nutmeg and golden pears does not exist. That is a conclusion we can arrive at on our own. There is, however, much knowledge to gain from them. I wonder if they could shed any light on the question if whether or not a tree falling in the woods makes a sound if there is no one around to hear it? Probably not.

There is a bit of information that is quite interesting regarding various trees. There is a disease that some trees are plagued with. It is a fungal disease that causes decay. The decay is at the center of the trunk and its branches. It is called heart rot and happens when fungi enter the tree by way of wounds in the bark. The tree then becomes prone to breakage because the wood is softened. Because of the rotting the tree is unlikely to survive. The tree should then be removed to prevent the spread to other trees.

The tree looks perfectly healthy from the outside, but there is a lot going on in the inside that is not seen. It is like the walls of a house being eaten up on the inside by termites, unseen from the outside yet the structure becomes so damaged that it renders no strength or support.

Put a human in place of the tree and think about the similarities. We can start by checking out how the heart rot begins. The culprit, the fungi, enters the tree through wounds in the bark. Those wounds can be caused by a variety of things such as broken branches, impacts, scrapes, abrasions and animal damage.

A person could suffer a wound in many ways, both physically and emotionally. Insults and degrading words can be very hurtful. Disparaging words, or speaking without thinking can easily cause hurt and distress. Proverbs 12:18 tells us of how speaking without thinking can cut like a knife. A quote from William Chapman says: "Words cut deeper than knives. A knife can be pulled out, words are embedded into our souls." Words penetrate deeply. There is no cure for the tree, but wise words can heal and thoughtful words can bring health.

The absence of wounds to the tree prevents fungi from entering. The absence of verbal wounds to us reduces hurt and harm, reduces stress and avoids adding another area in need of healing.

I Had A Little Nut Tree

The tree doesn't have much control over prevention from wounds and disease it may be afflicted with, we do. We can exercise some control, not complete control, of our surroundings, where we hang out, how and where we spend time, who our friends are, as well as our diet, and how, when and where we worship. There is a lot we can do to make life much better. There is guidance by way of God's Holy Spirit and His Word. We need to soak up both like a sponge. Soak it up to the point that it overflows to everyone around us.

Just like the tree, and the termite infested house, the internal destruction is not evident from the outside. We could do nothing for the tree, but there is much we can do for our brothers and sisters who may be hurting inside. We can only know if they hurt if they have enough faith and trust in us to share it with us. We must "Love thy neighbor as thyself" (Matthew 22;39) and reach out not lash out.

The disease causing hurt and internal harm can also be a result of diseased and misguided thinking. In both cases, the tree as well as our brother or sister becomes weakened, unsupportive, and eventually falls. A weakened brother can fall unless he gets our help and support. "Our" meaning us and God's Spirit within us. We cannot fix the problem by ourself, but we can and must be instrumental in guiding and pointing to the One who can.

Oranges and Lemons

Another traditional English nursery rhyme with much uncertainty as to its meaning. There is quite a wide range of possible meanings offered over the years with this particular nursery rhyme. From child sacrifice, public executions, to the marital problems of Henry VIII. There is reference to the bells of seven churches which adds to the uncertainty and confusion. Differences in churches remains today as each may ring their bells for various reasons as they did then and do today.

Oranges and Lemons was also the name of a dance back then, but there is also uncertainty whether or not there was any connection. Publication of this nursery rhyme was 1744. London had suffered through plagues and some believe that was another consideration for its writing.

Adding to the questionable meaning is a children's song of that time entitled Oranges and Lemons. The lines attached to the various churches mentioned in this does the same, each with its own reference and meaning. How many different churches do we have today? I would hope that they all, both then and now would ring there bells for the same reason, to signify time to gather for worship. That has remained consistent. It is the message within the walls of the various churches that has not. Some ring bells of jubilation and joy while others ring bells of ignorance because they have not concentrated and focused on the one true God, while altering and misinterpreting, and often ignoring the teachings of Jesus. Worship has become entertainment and Biblical principles modified to not offend fearing a reduction in attendance and giving. It has become commonplace to pick and choose based upon that which aligns more favorably to personal persuasion. Who is being worshipped? What is true and what is false when we here so many different bells ringing? Discernment is required to determine what is right and what is wrong.

Why oranges and lemons? Are they randomly chosen or were they chosen for a particular reason? Choices are made and too often the driving force, the motivating factor on which a choice is made is self propelled and self serving. There is often partial and total disregard for Truth, redefining and redirecting accordance, conformity, and compliance as deemed fit. It becomes clearer why there is so much confusion and misunderstanding as to which bell chimes correctly. Choices are made for the wrong reasons.

Oranges and Lemons was the name of a dance during a time when there was massive epidemics in England. (1603, 1625, 1636, 1665) including the Great Plague of London. Isn't distortion, omission, and misinterpretation of Scripture like a plague, an epidemic and even a pandemic?

Where do we go when we need clarity and understanding? We seek guidance from God and His Word. Through prayer and Bible study we can find both. There are several scriptures in God's Word that can help us. In I Corinthians 2:14 we read: "But a natural man does not accept the things of the Spirit of God, for they are foolishness to him; and he cannot understand them...". The Holy Spirit provides the ability to discern divine truth. It does not mean that everything is known, but we are given the ability to discern and gain clarity and understanding. Spiritually dead are unable to comprehend and discern.

We know there are both false and true teachings, several different bells are chiming. There are different beliefs and different proclamations. We need to discover and distinguish one from the other and determine which is based on the truth.

I want to quote five verses from the book of Matthew for further clarification. "Beware of the false prophets who come to you in sheep's clothing, but inwardly are ravenous wolves. You will know them by their fruits. Grapes are not gathered from thorn bushes nor figs from thistles, are they? So every good tree bears good fruit, but the bad tree bears bad fruit. A good tree cannot produce bad fruit, nor can a bad tree produce good fruit. Every tree that does not bear good fruit is cut down and thrown into the fire. So then, you will know them by their fruits." (Matthew 7:15-20)

Let the world know us by our fruits. By God's indwelling Spirit (Romans 8:11) the fruits of the Spirit will be manifest. The fruits of the Spirit are love, joy, peace, patience, kindness, goodness, faithfulness, gentleness, and self control. (Galatians 5:22-23)

Oranges and Lemons are not Spirit filled, they are not fruits of the Spirit, they are just fruits. People attending the various churches around the world can be seen in a similar way. A body of believers that is Spirit filled is not the same as a group of people where the Spirit is absent. A proclamation of Truth rings out from the church bells of one group. What we here from the other is simply ding dongs.

A Wise Old Owl

This rhyme refers to the traditional image that an owl is the symbol of wisdom. It was recorded in 1875 and believed to be much older, but the theme of wisdom being synonymous with owls has not changed. As a matter of fact, that is still the belief, unless you live in India. In India owls are associated with foolishness.

The wise old owl is described as not saying anything, just listening. We all could take a lesson from him in that regard. It would be wise for many to be quiet and listen more. The wisdom reputation is really not warranted according to many. The owl is a good hunter and has the ability to rotate its head so it can see better. They have tubular rather than round shaped eyes which prevents them from moving them around much. Hardly characteristics that would support the widespread belief that they are wise. Many believe the wise association to the owl was because Athena, a Greek goddess of wisdom, posed by holding an owl. In Greek mythology, a little owl traditionally either represented or accompanied Athena.

Greek mythology or simply put, myths were just that,

widely held but false beliefs. That may have contributed to the false belief of owls being wise. Let's look at how the word wisdom is defined.

The word "wisdom" is defined as the quality of having experience, knowledge, and good judgement; the quality of being wise." If there existed different bodies of knowledge, which there has been and there are, wisdom would be different from one body of believers to another. There are different belief systems, different sets of principles. Those different sets of principles form the basis of a religion, a philosophy, or a moral code.

In a mythology belief system, a make believe world, the origin and nature of the world could be made up, its fantasyland. In religion, the belief system must be of God not of man, otherwise it too would be made up.

The Bible, the infallible Word of God, tells us that the fear of the Lord is the beginning of wisdom. (Psalm 111:10) In Proverbs 1:7 we are told: "The fear of the Lord is the beginning of knowledge; Fools despise wisdom and instruction." An unbeliever, one who has not been born again and invited God into their life, may think they have knowledge, may comment on life and truth, but does not possess true knowledge.

A believer, born again, has a redemptive relationship with God. A buying back has occurred. That is reference to Christ dying on the cross. A relationship with Christ, the Son of God, sent to die for us, must exist in order to gain true knowledge. The truth is revealed to us through God's Word and His Spirit. Wisdom is having knowledge and also having the capacity to use it properly. It is acquired through experience. We grow and mature as we get closer to God and His truth is revealed to us.

There is only one valid and legitimate belief system and

that is directly from God. Any other is invalid and illegitimate. My heart aches for the people who have been misled and are held captive by a belief system that is not legitimate. Invalid belief systems are like many nursery rhymes, they are nonsense. A wise old owl would not give a hoot about nonsense, but would go to great lengths with efforts to help them become enlightened. We should be alert and aware, but also not be misled. We must be wise.

This rhyme tells of a wise old owl who spoke less with the more he saw, and the less he spoke the more he heard. The question is then asked; "why can't we all be like that wise old bird?" My question is this; Is it wise to not speak up when what you see is wrong? Are we to be silent and only listen to what we do not agree with? That doesn't sound like wisdom to me. Maybe India has it right. Is what we perceive as wise really more on the side of foolishness? When things are going in the wrong direction, it makes more sense to me to speak up and try to initiate some type of corrective action. Why would we turn our heads around 180 degrees like an owl and look away as if we don't see it? Is that wisdom?

A group of owls is called a parliament. A parliament is also a legislative body of government. Take a minute and think about that. Is our governing body wise or foolish? A governing body is a group of people who formulate policy which determines a recommended course of action. Should we follow a course of action recommended by man or one recommended by God? If the two are in alignment with each other the answer is easy. If they are not in alignment with each other what is the right thing to do? Wisdom says to base decisions upon truth and its author. "Therefore be careful how you walk, not as unwise men but as wise" (Ephesians 5:15) Wisdom is the ability to know what is true and right. Aligning our principles and beliefs with the One who laid the earth's foundation (Job 38:4) is truly evidence of wisdom.

Miss Polly Had A Dolly

A popular nursery rhyme in the United Kingdom which goes back to the late 19th century. It was often sung to children when they were sick. Miss Polly had a dolly that she thought was sick. She called the doctor and he went to her house. The doctor wrote a paper for a pill and returned the next day with the bill. The doctor made a house call and wrote a prescription. He did something that almost never happens by making a house call, and something that may happen too often with writing a prescription.

Many things change over time, they may get better, they may get worse. With some things there is little or no change. Let's put three things pertaining to this nursery rhyme under the microscope and try to determine what changes, if any, have taken place over the years, and whether those changes are good or bad. Those three things are the doll, the physician, and prescriptions.

A doll is basically a toy or a puppet that resembles a human. It has been loved and adored by many children and adults for a long time. Names have been given to them as if they were a part of the family. Many have been treasured and become an important part of collections. Dolls can be a precious companion or even a teaching tool.

There is also a darker side to dolls. Since ancient times, dolls have played a role in magic and religious rituals. They have been representatives of deities as well. Their use has been both positive and negative.

House calls by doctors and physicians have almost disappeared. The volume of individuals seeking care and cure for their ailments has increased. It is more practical, timely, and efficient to go to a physician rather than to have the physician go to each individual. That is a positive change.

A negative change may be that there exists access to many more drugs today and a dependence upon them may develop. Economic incentives may also have a role to play in some cases involving both physicians and prescriptions. Just as is the case with dolls, there can be both a positive and negative side to each. Without a doubt, the positive situations strongly outweigh the negative.

Regarding prescriptions, dependency, addiction, and illegal activity is a definite problem, but countless lives have been saved and countless lives are regularly administered to through a positive usage of prescribed drugs.

In all three examples, then and now, the determination of a positive or negative situation rests with the purpose and intent of the user. If and how something is used determines its affect and its effectiveness. Words can be used to build up someone as well as to bring them down. A hammer can be used the same way. It can be used constructively as well as destructively. If it remains unused in a toolbox it serves no purpose aside from being available if needed. An unused tool has no value and is of no benefit.

If miss Polly put her dolly on a shelf and never looked at it or never touched it, it would be of no value and no benefit. If a bottle of full of pills prescribed by a physician remained untouched in a cabinet or desk drawer, they too would be ineffective.

The same is true of the Bible, God's inspired Word. How many are on a shelf or in a drawer, never touched or looked at? A valuable tool neglected and unused. God's plan for humanity from beginning to end shelved and undiscovered.

Bible usage in America was documented in 2018. The findings are very interesting. The study was commissioned by the American Bible Society and conducted by the (Barna Group 2018). The study showed that half of Americans are Bible users and that 66% of Americans have some curiosity to know more about it.

Daily Bible usage was shown at 14%, once a week 8%, once a month6% and 3 to 4 times a year 8%. The number that speaks to me is 66%, two thirds of Americans have a curiosity and desire to know more about the Bible. What steps, if any, are taken by those people to learn more? Is the Bible left on the shelf because of misconceptions of its content? Has its use and interpretation also undergone a negative twist over time? Has the message from God been modified to be the message from man? A message to accept what you want, using it to justify anything you want to justify. Rejecting, ignoring or twisting anything necessary in an effort to support and uphold a desired way of thinking. People are confused and uncertain of where to go and what to believe. They are in search of answers. They want answers to truth, life, purpose and peace.

Miss Polly doesn't want a cracker, especially one that is spread with the variants of cheese the world has to offer. She too wants answers to the same questions. We all have questions. There is a curiosity and a desire within us to find truth and the meaning of life. Those questions within us have answers within the Bible, the Word of God, not the word of man.

We have become dependent upon a GPS to help us navigate from point A to point B. We feel a bit lost without it. The Bible is like a roadmap on the navigation of life. We definitely will be lost without the answers and message found within it. Unopened and untapped prevents the flow of truth, understanding, and freedom. The Bible is a collection of writings inspired by God's Spirit.

We must become more effective in helping people find answers. We need to help them with their curiosity to know more about the Bible. Miss Poly had a dolly that was sick and in need of a doctor. Our world has a sickness and is in need of a great physician who can provide the cure, make house calls anywhere, and who has already paid the price for the remedy. He and His teaching is the prescription for all of us.

The Bible is a key to unlock that truth. We need to play a key role in helping others use that key. Instrumental in encouraging them to open and discover, to seek and find Truth.

Hot Cross Buns

This is both an English Easter song and a nursery rhyme. It may surprise you that hot cross buns are a traditional sweet eaten on Good Friday. They are spicy cakes made with different kinds of fruits and decorated with a white cross. The bun marks the end of Lent, a time where Christians replicate the sacrifice of Jesus and His withdrawal into the desert for 40 days. A time of preparation before Easter celebration.

The spices inside the buns signifies the spices used in those days to preserve and give a pleasant fragrance in the preparation for burial.

There are other versions to this as well. There have been "not cross buns" where the cross is replaced by a smiley face, meaning not cross, but happy. Superstitions have arisen about keeping a bun for medicinal purposes, or even taking them aboard ships to offer protection against shipwreck. Fire protection by hanging them in a kitchen is yet another credulous belief.

There are rituals and traditions that undergo change over time. A ritual or a set of activities with a set sequence that must be followed is different from tradition, a belief or behavior that is passed on and that has a special significance to an origin in the past.

There was a change made with some buns being topped with a smiley face replacing the cross. Why the change? Was it to exclude or remove any reference to Christ and Christianity? Traditions can undergo changes very slowly and viewed as not significant. If changes are made gradually over a longer period of time, over generations, those minor changes can, and have become major changes. A gradual adjustment is made to new conditions and we are said to adapt to those new conditions, conditions that are suitable for a new use.

Replacing the cross is viewed as o.k. because it is simply an adjustment to current conditions which are actually, new conditions. New conditions suitable for a new use. What is that new use? It is a use that does not include Christ or any reference to Him.

"You leave the commandment of God and hold to the tradition of men." (Matthew 7:6-8) That gradual change may appear as insignificant, but it is very significant because it is an acceptance of moving further and further away from God and His commandments.

Within that distancing movement is the movement taking attention away from God and putting it upon self. That is evident in tradition, ritual and even in prayer and fasting. "When you pray, you are not to be like the hypocrites; for they love to stand in the synagogues and on the street corners so that they may be seen by men." (Matthew 6:5) "Whenever you fast, do not put on a gloomy face as the hypocrites do, for they neglect their appearance so that they will be noticed by men when they are fasting." (Matthew 6:16)

In both of those passages we are told not to be like the hypocrites, one who pretends to have certain beliefs, attitudes and feelings when they really do not. When self is elevated, raised to a higher level of importance or adoration, it becomes a matter of worshipping self and viewed as honor and reverence appropriately due. To worship ourselves is to express reverence and adoration as if we are a deity. There is only one true God and we are not it.

Traditions are beliefs or behavior passed on. There may be danger in modifying or changing some of them. Simply removing the cross from hot cross buns may have greater significance than we think.

There Was an Old Lady Who Swallowed a Fly

A rhyme and nonsense song also known as "I Know an Old Lady Who Swallowed a Fly." It is about an old woman who swallows increasingly larger critters or animals to catch the previously swallowed animal. She dies after swallowing a horse. Beginning with a fly and ending with a horse, obviously absurd and nonsensical, although humorous.

She died after eating a horse. I can't believe she ate the whole thing. Some people will swallow anything! Some people will believe anything. They believe and trust too readily. Those people are credulous, they have a willingness to believe without proper or adequate evidence. You know the type. Those who make up their mind and say, "that's that!" You cannot get them to listen to reason. They do not want to hear anything that may not allow them to go on with their life as they wish. They are hard headed and become close minded, refusing to believe anything that may require any change or adjustment in their self centered and self controlled life.

When all the signs and indicators say go that way, they will continue to go the other way. They are in denial, declaring something that is true to be untrue. Convinced in their own mind that the truth is not the truth and they continue on their own way.

Just as with the lady who swallowed the fly, what she swallowed got bigger and bigger until it killed her. The same progression, bigger and bigger and bigger happens to those who perceive the truth as untrue. The untruth gets bigger and bigger and bigger.

That trend is evident in our society today. There is less and less accountability and there is more of a widespread acceptance of just about anything. The result is a state of disorder and it is due to the absence or nonrecognition of authority. That is the definition of anarchy.

There is less and less recognition of God as authority. Each individual can nominate and elect themselves to the position of authority. That trend is obvious to many and ignored by many others. The difference between the two is some believe the truth and are unwilling to swallow anything and everything, while others feed on a never ending buffet of untruth.

God warns us through scriptures many times to be aware of, and to avoid false teachings. Correct and sound doctrine is crucial. It is critical to the success or failure of understanding the truth and to spiritual growth.

In addition to the verses in both Psalms and Proverbs telling us about the fear of the Lord being the beginning of knowledge and wisdom, there are many more scriptures that are both a warning and a reminder to stay alert. Chapter 2 in the book of 2 Peter tells us about destructive doctrines, false teachers and deceptions. "Many will follow their sensuality and because of them the way of truth will be maligned, and in their greed they will exploit you with false words, their judgement from long ago is not idle, and their destruction is not asleep." (2 Peter 2:2-3) False teachers and doctrine is still prevalent today, it has not fallen asleep, we have. This is a reminder to be aware and to stay alert.

The importance of seeking the truth and avoiding false and misleading teachings is mentioned often in the Bible because it is extremely important to avoid being gullible and a victim of deception. Additional scriptures include: "Beloved, do not believe every spirit, but test the spirits to see whether they are from God, for many false prophets have gone out into the world" (1John 4:1) "Beware of false prophets, who come to you in sheep's clothing but inwardly are ravenous wolves..." (Matthew 7:15) "I appeal to you, brothers, to watch out for those who cause divisions and create obstacles contrary to the doctrine that you have been taught; avoid them." (Romans 16:17) "For false christs and false prophets will arise and perform great signs and wonders, so as to lead astray, if possible, even the elect." (Matthew 24:24)

There are even more scriptures on this important topic. God inspired men like Peter, Paul, John and Matthew all wrote of the importance of being mindful of unsound doctrines, deception, false teachings and misinterpreted scripture. There was concern in their day, there is concern in ours. Seek the Truth and find the Truth. Feed on the Word of God not the word of man. Don't be one of those who bites off more than they can chew and seems to have a willingness to swallow anything. We can choke both physically and spiritually if we cannot digest and absorb into our system what we put into it. Choosing properly and wisely strengthens and supports our overall health. The quality of life is greatly impacted, on a physical and spiritual level by what we feed upon. Realizing that and acting upon it should be more than just food for thought.

Jack Be Nimble

This is quite a popular and familiar English nursery rhyme. Many have heard of how nimble and quick Jack was, much fewer know about jumping over candlesticks. Jumping candlesticks was a sport and a form of fortune telling. Clearing the candlestick without extinguishing the flame was considered good luck. There was an old custom of jumping over candlesticks at wedding feasts, a good jump was good luck, bad jump, bad luck.

There is a theory that connects Jack to the English pirate, Black Jack. Nimble referred to his illusiveness in escaping authorities in the late 16th century. Like so many old nursery rhymes there is a lot of uncertainty, but the most likely explanation is the tradition of candle jumping being a way of divining, or having supernatural or magical insight of future events.

Divination, or to be inspired by a god, is an attempt to gain insight into something. It may be a question or situation where insight is sought through ritual or an occultic process. Jumping over a candlestick would be as effective as rolling the dice, or throwing darts at a dart board where mystical or magical beliefs are the process used in gaining insight into anything. The ritual of jumping over the candlestick, or any action that simply follows a prescribed order without the divine intervention of the one true God is meaningless. Divine intervention is where God, or in the case of the simple and nimble minded Jacks of the world, a false god intervenes.

Intervention is "to come between", "get involved", or simply put, get in the middle of. Seeking insight from a false god instead of the one true God is ridiculous. Would you allow a lawyer to perform open heart surgery on you knowing that he or she aced the bar exam and had an exceptional talent of jumping over candlesticks? Of course not, he is not qualified. What qualifications allows a god from never never land to take the place of the God who made us? He created us and we still ship in numerous gods from fantasy island to take His place. There is one true Diety yet false gods are put in positions as if they have the attributes of the real one.

"All Scripture is inspired by God and profitable for teaching, for reproof, for correction, for training in righteousness" (2Timothy 3:16). Inspired by the one true God. Any teaching that is not in agreement and alignment with the Word of God is illegitimate regardless of how gracefully one does cartwheels, back flips, or candlestick jumping.

The Decalogue, the Ten Commandments are God given. Our Creator has given us a set of principles for our benefit. He wants us to live peaceful, happy, and productive lives. They are relevant today. One of those Commandments is "You shall have no other gods before Me" (Deut.5:7).

An unqualified person with false credentials is not going to be successful at his or her job. The end result will be inferior, inadequate and low in quality. We would not hire that person. We do not accept counterfeit money in place of the real thing, so why is there acceptance of counterfeit gods in place of the real thing? Something or someone imagined or supposed is not real.

Imagine trying to work at a job where there are too many claiming to be the boss, each having their own way of doing things and their own expectations. The result would be chaos and ineffectiveness. Little or nothing would get done. There can only be one boss. The saying "too many cooks spoil the broth" helps put things in perspective. Imagine a caravan of cooks from an imaginary place continuing to cook up nonsense stew. A stew that is a very popular menu item whose recipe is such that it not only spoils the broth, but ruins lives. The cooks think they are creating a delicious delicacy that we cannot get enough of. What they are actually cooking is their own goose. We could continue to eat that nonsense stew and we could keep jumping over a candlestick. You may be nimble and quick, but jumping over that candlestick you are likely to get burned.

Nonsense is more widespread and more prevalent than we may think. Attributing powers to imaginary gods, or jumping over candlesticks as a preventative measure, or as an indicator of ones fortune are just a couple of examples. Oftentimes it is not recognized. We see nonsense as just that, having no meaning or not making sense. It can be confusing or comical and to some it can be convincing.

Is it not nonsense to believe everything just magically happened to be put into place? Just by chance everything in the universe got aligned the way it is? The functions of the human body, with all its intricacies is the result of happenstance and is just a coincidence or an anomaly? That is nonsense that some believe. Things are so well designed there must be a designer. There is such organization there must be an organizer. Everything is orchestrated so well there must be an orchestra leader.

We have become so nimble minded, so quick to comprehend, yet some things remain mentally ungrasped. Why are we told to jump in the lake by those who are still jumping over candlesticks?

The Wheels On The Bus

An American folk song from the 1930's based on the nursery rhyme "Here We Go Round The Mulberry Bush." They share the same tune and are about daily activities or sounds that get repeated. Both are used as a teaching tool. Round and round, meaning around and around refers to habits repeated every day, the sounds made by certain things regularly, or over and over again.

We are creatures of habit and establish routines. Those routines are a regularly followed sequence of actions. They become fixed, sometimes deliberately, sometimes not. We go around and around as if in a circle repeating the same things over and over.

The circle affect differs from one person to the next, but there are many similarities. We could go around and around "chasing our tail" like a puppy who is entertaining himself. We could get caught up in a " vicious circle," a chain of events where one response to difficulty creates more and aggravates the original difficulty. Round and round we go.

We get preoccupied with an agenda devoted to provision.

We go to great lengths, spend a huge amount of time, and put forth much effort to maintain a supply line that enables us to have the necessities, or what we deem necessary for life. We must put food on the table, have a roof over our heads, have a mode of transportation, and so on. It is necessary to provide the means to make those things possible. That requires a continual effort to avoid interruption.

There are repercussions if that supply line is slowed or stopped. Commitments may not be able to be met. It may result in having to give up something. It may result in something being taken away. A cutting off of that supply line would create suffering or discomfort and could result in bankruptcy.

A disconnect from the supply line creates problems. It is no different with our spiritual well-being. We face the possibility of spiritual bankruptcy when we interrupt and cut off the supply line. While those wheels go round and round, our agendas must include devoting time for providing maintenance and preservation of our spiritual supply line. A direct line to God must remain open and be used on a regular basis.

Some see life as a circle, ashes to ashes, dust to dust. A phrase meaning humans are made from the dust of the Earth and their physical bodies will return to dust when the body dies. The physical body dies, but the spiritual body lives on, eternally.

Forever is a long time. In that period from dust to dust, how we spin our wheels is critical. Routines should be adjusted, and new ones established. The wheels on the bus go round and round, so do the hands of a clock.

I'm A Little Teapot

A song that is descriptive of the whistling sound of a tea kettle or the heating and pouring of a teapot. There is a distinction between teapot and tea kettle, but they are often used in place of each other. They both undergo a heating up process to reach a desired result.

A pot of water will heat up and, if left unattended, will reach the boiling point and boil over. The result is a mess which could have been avoided. A tea kettle will whistle and give us a warning if unnoticed or unattended. When we feel the heat and are about to reach our boiling point, wouldn't it be nice if we had some type of built in warning system, or something that could help us avoid getting to that point?

We put cooking oil inside the pan of water to prevent it from boiling over. Its presence works as a boiling point deterrent. God's Holy Spirit within us can do the same when we get angry and the pressure is building within us. His presence and guidance prevents us from going too far.

What is going too far? What is the meaning of Ephesians 4:26 "Be angry and yet do not sin?" We all get angry at some point. We should be angry with those who believe and spread things that are not true. Fabrications, falsehoods and lying are wrong and we should have strong feelings of disapproval and annoyance. We get angry but should not let it get to the point of boiling over which only creates more problems.

Even those who have God's Spirit within may struggle with anger and may question how that is possible. How can our pot boil over if it contains the necessary deterrent? The answer to that is because we push the deterrent aside and insist upon self control rendering the deterrent ineffective. We are quick to react upon things externally without involving the available resource of internal guidance. We continue to resort to the attitude of "I got this."

When we are standing at the stove and see a pot of water about to boil over, what do we do? We remove the pot of water from the heat and watch the water level go down. We have prevented a situation from getting out of control.

There are certain things that we can control and there are others we cannot. Avoiding a boiling point of emotions is one of those areas we need help with. If we can look at ourselves as being that pot of water close to the boiling point, who can remove us from the heat? We should take things to God and trust that He will guide us. If we do not, we are allowing that heat to increase and the pressure to mount. We know the result of that. Anger should not sit unresolved otherwise bitterness and vengeance may enter and grow. Removing ourselves from a concentration of what is causing the rising heat to a concentration of letting go and letting God is like the pot being removed from the burner.

Our anger must not be directed at individuals, but at the

untruthful and misguided banners which they wave. Forgiven people forgive people. Eruptions of anger and being overheated is not conducive to an atmosphere of forgiveness. It only contributes to the barrier we are trying to break down.

We are all like teapots, not all short and stout. Proper measures should be taken so what is desired is what comes out. It is much better to enjoy a cup of tea than to clean up a mess. What's your cup of tea?

Old MacDonald Had A Farm

One of the all time favorites about a farmer, the animals on his farm, and the sounds they make. I wonder how long Mr. MacDonald had his farm. If he had it as a young man, were the words originally "Young MacDonald Had A Farm?" We have come to associate the name MacDonald with golden arches and food. A place where there is plenty of oink, oink here and oink, oink everywhere.

What an awesome responsibility Old MacDonald had. Taking care of the growing and harvesting of various crops as well as caring for all of those animals. The farmer has dominion over the animals, or control and supreme authority over them. God gave man dominion over the animals at creation. (Gen 1:26-28) Being granted that authority separates man from the rest of the living creation and illustrates his unique relation with the rest of creation. Man was made in God's image. God has a unique relation to man and man has a unique relation to creation.

An analogy has been used of God creating Earth and then leasing it to man. The terms of the lease are God's terms. A foundation and a set of values, fundamental principles that He has established and represents. The terms of the lease are revealed through His Spirit and His inspired Word.

Failing to act in accordance with the "terms of the lease" is prevalent today. It is widespread and it is flourishing. It is viewed by many as acceptable and normal. Disobedience and defiance viewed as o.k. There is a daring and bold resistance to authority viewed as a right under the guise of freedom. The leaseholder is being ignored.

Old Macdonald had many animals on his farm. They all made a different sound and communicated within their own species. There was a moo, moo here, a quack, quack there or a cluck, cluck everywhere and so on. There are over 7000 human languages spoken today. Did you ever wonder why? Was it the result of disobedience, arrogance, and rebellion? A failing to act as expected or commanded? Was some kind of lease broken?

Take a look at Genesis 11:1-9 an explanation of the multiplicity of languages. A monument of pride was built by the post flood group lead by Nimrod, a great grandson of Noah. God made man, created as one with whom He could speak. There was one language, same language, same words (Gen 11:1). Led by Nimrod, this group was in the process of spreading out and populating the earth, being fruitful and multiplying, populating the earth abundantly (Gen 9:7) when they stopped at a place called Shinar. They decided to stop and build a city and a monument to their pride and for their reputation. They were disobedient, they were settling not scattering. This was also an act of rebellion displaying arrogance and pride. Their actions of building a monument in recognition of themselves, their abilities and their accomplishments was to put the spotlight on themselves, to glorify themselves not God.

Their actions resulted in language being confused, separation and a scattering over the face of the earth. (Gen 11:7-9). The tower of Babel as it is referred to, comes from a Hebrew word "balal" meaning "to confuse." As the scattering over the earth continued, a drifting in different directions resulted in a gradual drift linguistically as well. The linguistic drift can be quite a lengthy discussion, but I do want to touch on it.

We do know that Old MacDonald had a farm with many animals. If his farm was located in various places scattered over the face of the earth, animal sounds would be different in each area. A dog that says "woof woof" in English, says "wau wau" in German, "gav gav" in Russian and so on. The sound is the same, but its expression differs.

We hear the same word sounding a little bit different within our own country. There are different dialects and accents depending upon what part of the country you are in. How do you explain why someone from the south speaks differently than someone from the Midwest, or someone from New York or Boston sounds different from someone in Minnesota or even Canada?

Voices have been raised about the tower of Babel as an explanation of the multiplicity of languages being just a fanciful attempt or even a myth. It is looked at by some as another Biblical topic on a buffet of pick and choose to your liking. The view of the Bible being a buffet, of picking and choosing what you like and dispelling what you do not has spread over the years. There is a piece of farm equipment that has been used for many years, one that has been used to help spread that view, figuratively speaking, and is used very effectively in contributing to that view's growth and development. It is some type of spreader, you know the one.

There are different types of farming. Old MacDonald was a farmer who grew crops and raised livestock. A successful farm required a great amount of work, knowledge and care. He had many responsibilities, one of which was to act like a shepherd caring for his flock. Old MacDonald cared for his, and the Good Shepherd, Jesus takes care of His. (John 10:1-21) (Ps 23:1)

Crops grown on a farm require nurturing and care to enhance their growth. A healthy plant requires an elimination of weeds and diseases. That is done by one having an understanding and by managing the conditions necessary to healthy thriving plants. A good shepherd can help with that.

Old MacDonald had a farm, and on his farm he had a lot of responsibility. He had a lot of responsibility which required much watchful attention. We need much watchful attention and guidance on all of our farms. It is necessary in order for us to live healthy lives both physically and spiritually. Healthy lives by living by the truth and spreading the truth. A shout, shout, here. A shout, shout, there. Here a shout, there a shout, everywhere a shout, shout!

A Pinch of Salt

A short nursery rhyme with a simple message. A pinch of salt on a bird's tail will allow capture of the bird without fail. The rhyme itself is simple but getting close enough to a bird to put a pinch of salt on its tail is a different story. Perhaps it means that if you are close enough to put salt on the tail, you are close enough to capture it. Maybe we should just take that explanation with a grain of salt, or try and determine if the writer is worth his salt. If that has already occurred, would questioning it again be like rubbing salt in the wound?

Salt is used for more things than I realized. I knew it was used as a preservative, but I really just associate salt with something to put on French fries or popcorn. Besides being used as a preservative and flavor enhancer, it has been used in making soap, pottery and chlorine. It has been used in tanning as well as in bleaching and dyeing. There are a lot more uses for salt than I once realized.

With so many uses for salt, what did Jesus mean when He was delivering the greatest sermon ever, the sermon on the mount, and said: "You are the salt of the earth; but if the salt has become tasteless, how can it be made salty again? It is no longer good for anything, except to be thrown out and trampled under foot of men."? (Matthew 5:13)

He was speaking to His disciples and explaining to them that they, His followers and believers, will spread the Word and preserve the Truth. The Truth will be brought out and the their effectiveness enhanced by the Spirit within them. It could be said that Spirit filled followers of Christ tastefully preserve the Truth.

Pure salt cannot lose its flavor or effectiveness. Salt that is not pure will not work as a preservative and will have an undesirably flat taste. Salt that is lacking, is ineffective and of little use, perhaps only good for limiting growth on foot paths.

We generally associate salt with common table salt. It should be pointed out that there are impurities in table salt. It consists of approximately 85% sodium chloride and 15% made up of various minerals including magnesium, gypsum, and others. Compare that with the salt from the Dead Sea which is only approximately 30% sodium chloride and 70% other components.

Jesus was pointing out a difference between the effectiveness of one versus the other. We too have impurities, we are not perfect. A flavor indicates a distinctive taste. With God's Spirit dwelling within us our impurities are diluted and rinsed away making us capable of preserving the Truth and enhancing life.

If we are disciples and are to make disciples capable of preserving Truth while directing attention to how life can be enhanced with a distinct eternal flavor, we understand that any teacher "worth his salt" is able to inspire his or her students. Salt plays a crucial role in maintaining human health. In a time when we have so many irons in the fire, when there is so much on our plates, the salt of the earth can bring out the flavor and play a crucial role increasing awareness of a healthy spiritual life. The quality of things are better, more excellent, and more effective, when done in good taste. That is true both physically and spiritually. Enhancing and preserving requires a special ingredient.

Mary, Mary, Quite Contrary

Another English nursery rhyme with disputed religious and historical significance. There is a question of origin and to which Mary reference is made. Mary, the mother of Jesus; Mary, Queen of Scots, or Mary 1 of England?

There are also theories of what silver bells and cockle shells allude to. Attempts to explain what is meant by the question, "How does your garden grow?" have also been debated. There are various explanations depending upon which Mary is chosen in preference to the others. In each case, the question could be rephrased to ask " how are things going with all the things that are happening in your life?" Each Mary had a different set of circumstances in their time and their gardens did not look the same.

There are similarities in gardens and there are many differences as well. How gardens grow is determined by the steps taken and the effort made to make it grow well. Whether the garden is a reference to circumstances or an actual garden there are things we can do to assure a healthier environment for growth. How your garden grows is a reflection of your gardening habits. Neglected gardens are overgrown with unwanted weeds that have choked out or overrun potentially beautiful, flourishing plants. Beautiful gardens reflect cultivation to nurture and help plants reach their potential. The result of that cultivation is healthy plants that can blossom, thrive and grow vigorously.

Growing applies to us both physically and spiritually. Our physical health and vitality is greatly affected by the degree of nurturing and care given to it. Neglecting good habits and a continued absence of proper care can lead to undesired and unwanted physical conditions where the probability of continued deterioration is high. Life could be choked out. Practicing good habits and maintaining proper care helps prevent unwanted and undesired intruders.

Mental and physical health has a direct impact on quality of life. Being mentally and physically strong makes one better equipped to handle undesired and unwanted conditions. Being strong would help in deflecting, warding off or even preventing unwelcome intrusions by virus or disease.

"How does your garden grow?' may have been a question of the mental and physical condition of Mary in the midst of her circumstances. Was she holding up? Was she strong, was she struggling or was she ready to cave in? We have to make a continued effort to be strong in order to improve our quality of life. We must take the necessary steps to be healthy and strong mentally, physically and spiritually. We must cultivate the garden in all areas in order to blossom and thrive.

We know the physical practices and steps to take in order to achieve and maintain good health yet we are not very good at making them a habit. The same is true in regard to spiritual growth and health. If we are strong we are better equipped to ward off the enemy and avoid being led astray.

Just like the thriving plants in the garden, we must be fed in order to grow and mature. We "are no longer to be children, tossed here and there by waves and carried about by every wind of doctrine, by the trickery of men, by craftiness in deceitful scheming, but speaking the truth in love, we are to grow up in all aspects into Him..." (Ephesians 4:14-15) We cannot grow if we are not fed properly. We must prevent weeds from growing in our garden so we can blossom.

A blossom is a flowering part of a plant that forms seeds and fruit. Our gardens should be full of blossoms, vigorous and thriving. In order for that to happen our lives must show that we belong to God by faith in Christ and that we possess the Spirit of God. The evidence of His Spirit living within us are the attributes known as the fruits of the Spirit. "But the fruit of the Spirit is love, joy, peace, patience, kindness, goodness, faithfulness, gentleness, self control..."(Galatians 5:22-23). These qualities of Christian behavior are the result of believers submitting to the guidance of the Holy Spirit dwelling within them. Our attributes should resemble those fruits. If they do not, our actions are likely to be inclined to do the opposite of what is expected or desired. That inclination of being opposite in nature and direction is being contrary. Mary was quite contrary. Her garden almost certainly reflected that. Bitter fruit is a result of being rooted in bitterness. Good roots, good fruit.

Going against what is natural and what is expected and

desired makes us contrary and our gardens will also reflect that. If we align with what is natural and what is expected and desired by our Creator our gardens will flourish, fruits will be abundant, life will be abundant. How does your garden grow?

Little Jack Horner

Yet another nursery rhyme involving Jack. This was written as a satirical poem. There have been various targets throughout history that this may allude to, including Thomas Horner who was a contemporary of Henry VIII. It seems that Mr. Horner delivered a Christmas pie to Henry VIII. It was not your typical pie in that there was something hidden within it. There were deeds to a dozen manors inside. This happened at a time when Henry VIII was closing monasteries and seizing their properties. He had broken from the Catholic Church and took the opportunity which had presented itself.

The pie has since been a reference to opportunism, especially in politics. Mr. Horner stole one of the deeds. This rhyme may have been written as a satirical reference to the dishonest actions of Mr. Horner. This was happening at a time known as the Tudor period in England, a time of great change including the decline of the Catholic church.

Opportunism or the taking of opportunities when they arise, can be done in an honest and upright manor but is all too often practiced with little or no regard for honesty or what is appropriate. Opportunism often brings out greediness, selfishness, and a concern for your own welfare disregarding the welfare of others. Jack was in a corner as if not wanting to be seen by others, he pulled out a plum as if it was a prize and reward for his efforts. He did not have to share with anyone because there was no one around to share with. That was most likely deliberate.

Crimes of opportunity are committed on a regular basis. Many have become experts at it. The greatest opportunist is Satan who specializes in crimes of opportunity. He has many tools in his trade and is a master craftsman, highly skilled in his craftiness. Skilled in deception, sly and cunning, ready to pounce at any opportunity that presents itself.

The quality of our lives, now and forever, is determined by our choices. We can choose to align with God or choose not to. Choosing to align with God we surrender our hearts to Him and try to stay in alignment with Him. In that effort we are constantly confronted by our enemy, our adversary, the opportunist specialist, the prowling lion. "Be of sober spirit, be on the alert. Your adversary, the devil, prowls around like a roaring lion, seeking someone to devour." (1Peter 5:8)

The tools of pettiness and deceitfulness are used continuously in an attempt to obstruct, divert and derail. Keep your path from being blocked and diverted. Be an opportunist and take advantage of the opportunity God has made available to us. His open arms await. Instead of going into hiding and choosing to not be seen or heard as a result of opportunism of a questionable nature, come out and be seen and heard. The opportunity for a joyful everlasting life is far more rewarding than a plum. The right choice should be very obvious. The wrong choice is just plum crazy.

Twinkle, Twinkle, Little Star

Twinkle, twinkle, little star, how I wonder what you are! Originally written as a poem by the same author as far back as 1806. The lyrics help paint a picture of something we all have done. Gazing into the sky, up above the world so high, amazed by the diamond like twinkling of the vast amount of stars, wondering about so many things. Somewhat mesmerized by the amazing sight, we become transfixed by the beauty and slip into wonderland. Wondering about what is out there, Is God looking down at us, did He create us, what is beyond this life, and on and on.

Gazing up into the unknown we may ask how is it possible to know all the stars by name? The Bible tells us that: "The infinite God knows the stars by name." (Psalm 147:4) He created the heavens and the Earth. We are told that in the very first verse of the very first book in God's inspired Word. From the very first verse to the last verse in the book of Revelation, a collection of 66 documents inspired by God, there is a revelation of who God is. There is a unifying theme of Scripture. God created mankind and those who praise, honor and serve Him will be components of His kingdom. To those His power, mercy, grace, and glory is displayed.

The answers to many questions are found when we embrace both God and His Word. I have read many times the words: "we were created on purpose, for a purpose." When there is a companionship between man and his Creator a bond exists where elements of separation dissolve. Many things are made clearer and the closeness increases as the walk together continues.

Some questions will remain because our finite mind cannot comprehend the infinite mind of God. We are reminded to lean not unto our own understanding (Proverbs 3:5-6) to trust in Him and He will direct our paths. Following that path we grow in knowledge and understanding.

As we continue to gaze at the stars, up above the world so high, shining like diamonds in the sky, we may wonder about how, what, where, and why as if we are somehow connected to what is beyond the physical world as we know it. Wondering of such things as how we were made, why we were made or what does it mean being made in the image and likeness of God?" (Gen 1:26-28)

That question has been debated by philosophers and theologians for over a thousand years. Several explanations and definitions have been offered and expressed over quite a long period of time in the attempt to provide clarity and understanding. What does it mean to be created in the image and likeness of God? Does it mean man is God's representative in ruling over and having dominion over His creation? Is it the ability to exercise free will and reason? Is it the ability to have a relationship, or the ability to have knowledge, righteousness and holiness? Is it our psychological or spiritual makeup? Is it having moral attributes? Is it consciousness and the ability to speak? It could be some or all of those, the questions seem to be as plentiful as the stars.

We should not stumble and get caught up in the pursuit and definition of God's image and likeness but instead be defined ourselves, by our pursuit of Christ likeness. In that pursuit, the image and likeness of God will be made manifest.

There is a guiding light amongst all the darkness and we should not use a dimmer switch to minimize its brightness. The stars shine above the world so high like diamonds in the sky. The world we live in needs to see us shine brightly like a diamond in the rough. Twinkle, twinkle, little star.

Blow Wind, Blow

This rhyme has to do with the use of windmills in the making of bread. The windmill goes back at least as far as the year 1185 which was the earliest written record indicating its use. Many windmills were powered by rivers and many by the use of the wind.

The wind can be used for many things, in both a positive and negative sense. It can be used to power a windmill or a sailboat, it can be used to pump water for irrigation or even generate electricity for homes and business. Wind power in the U.S. produces around 5% of our electricity. There are many uses of wind, even in making bread.

The wind blows, the mill goes. The corn is ground until flour is found. The baker takes it and into rolls makes it. A positive change takes place. Just like the transformation from milk, to butter, to cheese. Something can start one way and end up quite different. That change is not always positive. The transition from corn into bread is a controlled and an intended change, as is milk to butter. A positive change. The transition from this to that is not always positive nor is it always controlled.

A beautiful beach house may end up as a pile of rubble if the waves, with their soothing sound, erode the beach and cause it to collapse. That is an example of a negative change that may or may not have been controlled. The wind has the ability to change the surface of the Earth by what is known as wind erosion. It can also degrade soil structure, lower water holding capacity, and reduce crop production. There are natural transitions and there are those that are caused by our activity, or lack of it.

When the wind is empowering our windmills, our generators, or simply providing a cool breeze on a hot summer day, it is very welcome. We might find ourselves saying; blow wind, blow. It is not welcome when it is so strong that it threatens to blow the roof off of our house, or creates sandstorms, or erodes our foundations. We should be alert to the threat of negative impacts and changes and not be like little boy blue, as we will learn more about later, who was fast asleep in a haystack unaware of impending danger. In many instances the horn needs to be blown to bring notice to potentially dangerous situations and to indicate any impending danger. We should pay attention to the wind, how strong it is, where it is coming from, and what it may be blowing our way. The wind blows notions to accept the changing of standards. The change from one to none is viewed as freedom and progress. One standard is viewed as too limiting so a double standard must mean it's twice as good. How did these misguided attitudes get so much wind under their sails?

Our attitudes are settled ways of thinking that is reflected in our behavior. They should not be influenced by strong winds of deception and misrepresentation. The impending danger that blows from the mouths of the mentally and spiritually blind must have the propelling winds in their sails stopped. Gusts of deception disguised as reason and comfort continue to fill the sails of many. Those winds have a mind numbing effect resulting in a slow drift meandering off in the wrong direction.

We take action to prepare and stay out of harms way from the damaging winds of hurricanes and tornadoes. The necessary action should also be taken to avoid the damaging winds of the unknowing, misguided and misinformed. Earlier I had referenced Ephesians 4:14. It needs to be repeated for emphasis. "Then we no longer be infants, tossed back and forth by waves and blown here and there by every wind of teaching and by the cunning and craftiness of people in their deceitful scheming." Lies so clever they sound like the truth are continually swirling around us.

If we are sleeping in a haystack like little boy blue, or run and hide in a boat like Jonah, we stand to lose more than a roof or a beach house. When you realize what is stake, efforts to do something about it should be done with great enthusiasm and effort. Prepare and be aware, put your heart and soul into it, literally.

Simple Simon

Simple Simon was just that. This nursery rhyme first published in 1764 is about the escapades of a simpleton named Simon. His actions like fishing in a pail, or looking for a plum on thistles, indicates that he was a bit foolish and gullible. The origin of the name Simon is Hebrew and the meaning is "the listener." The simple solution to many problems is to listen. Just as important is who we listen to. There are others of interest who shared the name of Simon whose surroundings and experiences were quite different than those of Simple Simon.

Simon, a man from Cyrene was a man who was compelled, "pressed into service" to carry the cross of Jesus as he was taken to his crucifixion. People who were sentenced to death in those days, had to carry their own crosses to where they were to be crucified. The soldiers of the Roman government, who had beaten and mocked Jesus, told Simon to bear His cross.

Take a little time to let this sink in. Of all the people in the world, since Creation, one man named Simon was the one who carried the physical cross of the Son of God. A defining moment? Certainly an impressive thing to have on a resume or a list of accomplishments, but an important question needs to asked. What was the motivation to pick up the cross? Scripture tells us that Simon was told to do it. (Matthew 27:32) What if he responded with great willingness and without hesitation, eager to assist? Maybe he wanted to but held back. Did he refrain from taking action without being told because of fear of repercussion? Did he respond only because he was told to do so and did he do it reluctantly? Did he respond out of fear or did he want to help but was waiting for the appropriate time?

Another Simon, the brother of Andrew, was one of the 12 apostles and a leader among them. His name Simon (Greek) or Simeon (Hebrew) was changed to Peter (Greek) or Cephas (Aram.) both meaning stone or rock. The reason for the change from Simon to Peter is of very great significance.

Jesus changed Simon's name to Peter. When Jesus asked His disciples; "Who do people say that the Son of Man is?" The answers included John the Baptist, Elijah, Jeremiah or other prophets. When Jesus asked; "But who do you say that I am?" Simon answered "You are the Christ, the Son of the living God." (Matthew 16:13-19) Jesus then told Simon that his answer was revealed to him by "My Father, who is in heaven" and that "you are Peter, and upon this rock I will build My church…"

The apostles played a foundational role, a very key role in building the Christian church. The recognition of Jesus, the Architect, Builder, Owner and Lord of the church as part of the "Oneness" of God, is the foundation of the church. The church is made up of the "called out ones" (Greek for church). Simon/Peter recognized and accepted Jesus, vital, essential, absolutely necessary to building the church, the Kingdom of God.

Simple Simon

If you could change your name to Peter, which would be most descriptive of you? Would you be gullible, uncaring, or not interested, attaching no importance to the subject of church or Jesus? Maybe you would choose to be one that does things only because you are told and just go through the motions. Maybe you would be eager to pick up the cross, make sacrifices for others and gladly contribute to spreading the gospel. Would your role be that of an actor or that of a key person, a supportive person?

There is a children's game that most of us played as a child called Simon Says. A game where instructions are given and only to be followed if prefaced with the words Simon says." We should pay more attention to what God says than what Simon says. Isn't that simple, Simon?

Old Mother Hubbard

An old English rhyme published in 1805 that most of us have heard many times. The tale of an old woman going to her cupboard to get her dog a bone only to find it empty. Once again, as with many rhymes, there have been alterations and origin questions.

A popular interpretation claims that it is in reference to Thomas Worsley (1686-1750) an English academic and priest who, unsuccessfully attempted to get an annulment for Henry VIII. The bone was in reference to the annulment sought for the marriage between Henry VIII and Katherine of Aragon. The certainty of that, as is often the case concerning old nursery rhymes, remains in question.

Mother Hubbard's cupboard was empty. A cupboard is a cabinet where things are stored. Mother Hubbard found no bone there for her dog nor was there an annulment for Henry to be found. We can't keep everything in our cupboards. We cannot go to our cupboards thinking they are filled with everything we could ever want or need. They do not contain everything nor are they labeled as such.

Is there anywhere we could go where "ANYTHING" could be obtained? Matthew 21:22 says; "And all things you ask in prayer, believing, you will receive." The gospels tell us to "ask and it will be given to you…" (Luke 11:9 Matthew 7:7) So, what exactly does that mean? Does it mean I will get the winning lotto ticket if I ask for it in prayer? What about praying for my favorite team to win? If someone else pulling for the other team is praying for their team at the same time, how is that resolved? There must be conditions or guidelines or further explanation needed to get clarity with this.

The best starting place to gain clarity is with our Creator, the Creator of the universe, take it to God in prayer. Prayer is communication with God, a way of sending or receiving information. God gives us what He wants us to have. What is in the cupboard is what He allows us to have. It is not stocked with selfishness, pride, disrespect, deceit or anything that does not align with His nature.

What it is stocked with is what we can discover by opening that cabinet. It is so true that we are able to ask and it will be given to us, to seek and to find, but we need to knock and see what God has in store for us by opening the door of His cabinet and by opening our hearts and minds.

Many of our own cabinets are bare and we go there in search for the wrong things. What God has in store for us is far greater than anything we can stockpile on our own. Read Matthew 6:19-21, "Do not store up for yourselves treasures on earth, where moth and rust destroy, and where thieves break in and steal. But store up for yourselves treasures in heaven, where neither moth nor rust destroys, and where thieves do not break in or steal, for where your treasure is, there your heart will be also."

When mother Hubbard went to her cupboard or cabinet she did not find what she was looking for. What exactly are you looking for? Do we look for the wrong thing when we ask God for a winning score, or a winning lottery ticket even if we believe we have more faith than that of a mustard seed?

The word "cabinet" comes from the Italian word "cabinetto" which means a small private room. It was descriptive of a good place to communicate without being interrupted. When we communicate with God in prayer, a private place without interruption is recommended, although we can pray anywhere, anytime. When we are in prayer, in that private place where there is a direct line of communication, we can sense that we are in the presence of God, a holy place, a place that is pure and full of all that is upright and good. A place that is indicative of the contents of His "cabinet." We need to open those cabinet doors and leave them open, not just opening them for a search that is purely selfish. Instead of looking for a winning lotto ticket we will find a winning ticket to life. Mother Hubbard's cupboard was bare, her cabinet was empty. God's cabinet is full. Open it.

Little Boy Blue

A call to come blow your horn little boy blue because the sheep are not where they're supposed to be and neither is the cow who is in the corn! Published in 1744, it is believed to be much older, possibly going back to the middle ages (1100-1453).

A person known as a "hayward" or a "hedge warden" was someone in charge of fences and enclosures having duties of a herdsman in charge of the animals. Little boy blue had the responsibility of watching over the animals like a shepherd looks over his sheep. He used his horn to warn or direct the animals as needed.

Evidently. he shirked his responsibilities in favor of a nap under a haystack. He must have been a bit wimpy because no one would wake him in fear of him crying. Obviously, he didn't take his job too seriously and didn't want to be bothered. That sounds familiar, pretty commonplace today. All we need to do is look around and we'll see the same behavior of putting what we want over what we should be doing. Calling those people out seems to make them wine and cry while screaming how mean and inconsiderate you are for interrupting and interfering with their personal agenda.

Little boy blue needed to blow his horn to get things back in order. Things were not the way they were supposed to be. Who's going to blow the horn for us today? Chicken Little is too old and the sky isn't falling, besides he just created a panic. The boy who cried "wolf" is long gone too. I'm sure he has relatives that could do the same thing, but everyone would assume it was a false alarm and they wouldn't pay any attention to them, it would fall on deaf ears.

A lot of selective hearing going on. Some only hear what they want to hear even if the message is life changing and a matter of life and death. Many ears do not hear because of an ear infection caused by misconception, misinterpretation and deception. We must not be discouraged by those who refuse to listen. We must continue to let the sound of Truth ring out so ears may hear. "Truly, truly, I say to you, he who hears My word, and believes Him who sent Me, has eternal life. Truly, truly, I say to you, an hour is coming and now is, when the dead will hear the voice of the Son of God, and those who hear will live." (John 5:24-25)

The sheep are in the meadow, the cows are in the corn, the chickens have flown the coop and there are bats in the belfry. It's time to let the cat out of the bag and reveal the facts to those from which they have been hidden. It's not time to sleep under the haystack. It's time to wake up and blow your horn!

Hide and Seek

Hide and seek is not a rhyme, it's a game. A game is a structured form of play. Play is engaging in an activity for enjoyment. Some people see life as a game, engaging in activities solely for self edification, preoccupied with themselves and their affairs. We have all heard the phrase, "the game of life." Many view the game of life as living by a set of rules or values based on worldview and beliefs. Those views and beliefs differ. Each thinks their rules are right and true. Who is right?

There can only be one set of rules that is right, being morally good and justified. There can only be one belief system that is true, or in accordance with fact and reality, that aligns with God. There is only one belief system that passes all the tests to qualify as legitimate, the real deal.

To reach that conclusion one cannot hide from the truth, they must seek it. The greater effort made in seeking the truth, the more truth will be discovered. A belief system must consist of truth. When seeking the truth in a court of law a witness put his or her hand on the Bible and was asked if they swear to tell the truth, the whole truth, and nothing but the truth, so help you God? Why the Bible and help from God? Because God is great, God is good. He is the Creator and ruler of the universe. He is the source of all moral authority. Absolutely the supreme being. A belief system that does not align with God, the one true God, is flawed.

Life has been described as a journey. As we make this journey, God should be at the center of it. Why would anyone choose an alternate mode of transportation? An unwillingness to relinquish control of the wheel can lead us down the wrong roads and down pathways that can be harmful, detrimental, or worse. Every path has a destination. Are we insistent on our own way or His way? There seems to be decreasing belief in the golden rule and clichés like "if it's worth doing it's worth doing right." Not caring is for those like Jimmy whose corn is not the only thing cracked. Their foundation is cracked.

Hiding from the truth and taking an alternate mode of transportation does not make sense. Seeking the truth and finding it will set us free. (John 8:31-32) A freedom from not being imprisoned or being held captive by flawed belief systems, freedom from sin, and a freedom from searching for reality. Reality is a state of things as they actually exist. Truth is found by believing in Him and His teaching, and by continuing in His Word. There is no longer a need to search for truth anywhere else because it is found in Him. We are free from the searching and thereby have a passion to share the Truth and the good news. In the game of hide and seek players can remain hidden or they can come out of hiding and race to home base and be free by touching it. In the game of life we can become free by returning home to the home base of our Creator. By reaching out and touching Him.

Hide and Seek

We get so preoccupied by trying to win the game of life that we do not allot enough time and energy to our Creator, putting Him on hold until we can squeeze Him into our busy schedules. How long can we remain on hold until we are cut off?

Our mentality, our mindset, our philosophy of life is shaped by our belief system. It is paramount that we accept and embrace the only one that is real. The only one that is from the one true God. There is a freedom that cannot be adequately expressed in words, a peace that fills heart, mind and soul. It only comes from one place and that is from the indwelling Spirit of God, the author of Truth.

The game of hide and seek is played by children who are growing and not yet fully developed. It is also played by adults who's sense of truth and reality has not matured and fully developed. Winning the game of life comes from seeking and finding the Truth, not hiding from it. Seek the Truth, find the Truth, and live the truth. We must ask ourselves this question; do we Hide or do we Seek? In the game of life and in the game of hide and seek, when the counting is over and the time is up, we can expect the same… " Ready or Not, here I come!

Happily Ever After

I hope you found this interesting and informative, arousing curiosity and interest, holding or catching your attention. Its intent was to encourage the reader to take a look at the direction of your heart. In the beginning we looked at four words. They were looked at in an order that deviated from the normal order, or the original order. That was done intentionally. When things are out of order, the natural flow is disrupted. Fee, Fie, Foe, Fum flows better than Foe, Fee, Fie, Fum . On a grander scale, the same is true regarding the natural alignment set into place by God. Disruption and disorder occurs when that natural alignment is altered and modified and when efforts are made to replace it.

Changing the order of the words in the beginning may have been so subtle that it went unnoticed. As things are changed little by little, piece by piece, and are not noticed, or seen as being trivial or of no great significance, a breaking down and erosion continues. A crumbling of a foundation occurs gradually, unnoticed. It is time to take notice and do something about it.

The writing of this book, the entire body of work was done

in an effort to be helpful, encouraging, and enlightening to the reader regarding the importance of our connection with our Creator and the foundation He has established. There needs to be an awareness of the disconnect that is taking place. The movement away from God needs to be changed to a movement closer to God. A life where God is not invited to be a part of is in tremendous contrast to a life led aligned with God and His principles and maintained by staying in tune with His Holy Spirit. A life with Him results in an abundant life now and forever.

The theme of this writing is to bring attention to how things are as opposed to how they could be. An attempt at bringing an awareness to how things can be spun in such a way as to sway one to a desired belief. It makes no sense to deviate from the one who put things in motion in the very beginning. It could be said that the intent is to increase focus upon how God put things in order, the original spin. and decrease focus of what is being spread as a result of original sin. There is a lot of nonsense in spins that go off in a different direction. We need to draw nearer to God, not get farther away from Him. Greater effort needs to be put forth to gain understanding and closeness to Him.

God is Spirit and we cannot reduce Him to our physical level in trying to understand Him. We can communicate with Him on a spiritual level and invite Him to dwell within us resulting in enlightenment and understanding. With Him we can remain aligned and in tune. Fee Fie Foe Fum, the gospel is for everyone. The truth is the truth and cannot be rewritten yet attempts have continued since the first apple was bitten. I have not written this with no rhyme or reason, but have done so driven because of the season. It's time to awake, assess and adjust. Awakening and action is absolutely a must. Being held captive by one so clever, is a high price to pay that could last forever.

Living happily ever after is possible and it can begin now. That can only happen if our heart is surrendered to Him and is directed to Him and by Him. A relationship with our Creator can be a reality. It is not a negative thing in that life must adhere to rules and regulations. It is positive in that His Spirit can dwell within us and enrich and empower us, improving and enhancing the quality of life.

We have looked at several nursery rhymes, most surrounded by a lot of uncertainty as to origin and meaning. That uncertainty leaves the door open for freedom of interpretation. A freedom to pick and choose that which is preferred over other interpretations. One will have a tendency to pick that which aligns with, or supports any given position. Origin and meaning then become optional, allowing for selection of the most desirable among any number of alternatives. The basis and foundation upon which that choice is made is done arbitrarily. There then becomes no need to have a foundation of truth, but rather one of unrestrained personal whim. Reality is set aside, nonsense can be embraced. Any project taken on has a much better chance for success when being properly equipped. Our life experience is no different. Aligning with the One who created us puts us in a place where there is none better, we embrace reality and discard nonsense.

The position taken regarding both the origin, and the meaning of life should not be based upon anything other than the truth. The truth should be sought after. A modified version of the truth is not truth, yet we continually allow it to be viewed as such. Seeking the truth and finding the truth, not a substitute for it, is the only way we can live happily ever after.

The only way to find the truth is to seek it. We cannot be satisfied with man made spin offs, or byproducts requiring obligation and commitment to those who create them. Artificial flavoring is a substitute for the real thing. We can only find truth by seeking it from its Creator, our Creator, the Author of truth. "Ask and it will be given to you; seek and you will find; knock and it will be opened to you." (Matthew 7:7) Seek it, Find it, Live it, happily ever after. Forever is a long time, try wrapping your mind around that. "Truthful lips endure forever, but a lying tongue is but for a moment." (Proverbs 12:19) Find truth, live happily forever after.